Jesus has given me joy and purpose in living.

Mildred Tengbom

THE BONUS YEARS

MILDRED TENGBOM

Presented by Crusaders Class

AUGSBURG PUBLISHING HOUSE
Minneapolis, Minnesota

ACKNOWLEDGEMENTS

Thank you:

To the many who worked with me in group discussions, and especially to the 30 or 35 in Long Beach and Garden Grove who worked with me for 8 and 12 weeks

To those who answered questionnaires

To those whose stories are contained in the book

To Dr. Marge Wold, Dr. Georgia Olson, Dr. William E. Bingham, Mrs. Alice Wright, Rev. Martin Olson, Rev. Charles Endter, and Miss Viola Blake for reading and critiquing portions or all the book

To my husband, Luverne, to Dan, Judy, Janet, and David who constantly encourage and cheer me on

To my editors and fellow-workers at Augsburg

THE BONUS YEARS

Copyright © 1975 Augsburg Publishing House

Library of Congress Catalog Card No. 74-14180

International Standard Book No. 0-8066-1463-3

Scripture quotations unless otherwise noted are from the Revised Standard Version of the Bible, copyright 1946, 1952, and 1971 by the Division of Christian Education of the National Council of Churches.

Quotations from the Living Bible, copyright 1971 by Tyndale House Publishers are used by permission.

Manufactured in the United States of America

Contents

Preface

Today's smaller families and the better health we enjoy as a result of medical care and research have gifted us a longer span of middle years than has ever been known before by a generation or civilization. The years between the birth of the first child and the day the last one leaves home are only about half the length of the marriage. The remaining years of lessening family responsibilities and increased freedom while health still is good become indeed *the bonus years*. For many this lengthened middle years span becomes a time of crisis, full of threat, full of risk. But inherent in that crisis are opportunities also, a chance to try something new or untried.

In my personal research I met with groups of people from three churches for varying lengths of time. We batted around the subjects discussed in this book, shared experiences, offered insights. I also sent questionnaires to about 80 people. From all these contacts, from extensive reading of books related to the thesis of this book and also from the experiences of previous years I have drawn for illustrative material for the book.

In relating the stories of others, when I do not use a surname you will know I am using fictitious names as anonymity was requested. But all the stories are true. Browse among them. Try them on for size. Some may offer insight and help.

Come, then, and join me as together we consider the problems and opportunities of the middle years, the bonus years. If we face them with God, we can declare with confidence, "The best is yet to come!"

Have I Lived My Life Right?

*The middle years are like New Year's.
It's an age to think about what you've
done up till now, and what you ought
to do in the future.*
— ERIC BERNE

"I was running, running, running," David Rothschild said. "Running because I was afraid to slow down to think. I feared I might discern my goals were not as meaningful as I, a successful real estate broker, had thought."

At middle age the questions were there in David's heart, crying out for an answer. But he kept pushing them back, becoming busier and busier so he would not have time to think.

Re-ordering Our Lives

It happens to almost all men, usually between the ages of 39 and 42—and sometimes later—according to Yale psychologist, Daniel Levinson. He drew his conclusion after a three-year study of males, aged 35 to 45. Questions arise, questions man faced once before in his adolescence. Now he faces these questions as a mature person, one who has had an opportunity to test what he thought he believed in. At about the same time in life, women, too, begin to face these questions.

The questions probe: Who am I? Why was I born? What is the meaning of life? What have I accomplished? What will I be remembered for? What will happen to me after death? Has life been worth the hassle?

The questions will come even to those who have been successful in their work and love lives. Some, faced with the questions, collapse into a state of confusion and chronic introspection regardless of past achievements. Others go on to a whole new life.

It is highly important that we find satisfying answers. If we don't, we will sink into cynicism, despair, indifference, lassitude, crankiness, or bitterness. We also will not be able to move along to satisfy the basic needs of our next span of life, old age, which lies immediately ahead.

For every age span in life has its own unique developmental tasks. Erik H. Erikson has defined them: (1) early infancy: trust; (2) later infancy: autonomy; (3) early childhood: initiative; (4) middle years of childhood: industry; (5) adolescence: certainty of self, sense of continuity and belonging regarding career, sex role, and a system of values; (6) early adulthood: intimacy; (7) middle adulthood: generativity or expansion of interests and a sense of contributing to the future; (8) late adulthood: ego integrity or the basic acceptance of one's life as having been meaningful.

The middle years offer us, if we need it, a second chance, a time to reorder our lives, to begin to live differently so at the end of life we shall be able to look back with satisfaction and be ready to die with peace and serenity.

How did it work out for David Rothschild?

"I was running, running, afraid to stop and think," David said. "And then suddenly I was hauled up short in my pursuit of money, success, and pleasure, for my son, my only son, was in trouble.

"Hooked on methedrine. Shooting up with heroin. 'Tripping' with LSD. This led to burglary, car theft, heavy drinking. For five years I existed in a living hell. Three times, shame washing over me, I heard the judge commit my son to juvenile jail.

"To pay lawyers, doctors and psychiatrists I had to work more frantically than ever. Yet all the time disturbing questions kept nudging me: Was this all there was to life? No more meaning than this? Troubles, sorrow and then the grave?

"I began to drink. I planned exciting vacations. My wife and I filled our social calendar. I pushed the sale of more houses.

"My son's condition worsened. He was committed to a state hospital. When the doctor dismissed him, the doctor said they could do nothing more for him, that I should never expect him to be a productive adult. I felt worse than ever. I didn't know where to turn. No matter what authority I had appealed to, none could give me hope. I wished life would end."

David ordered his son to find a job. The woman at the employment bureau referred David's son to a woman who, she thought, could help him. He went to see her.

A short while later the phone in David's home jangled. It was his son. "I've prayed to receive Jesus," he announced. "My sins are forgiven."

"I thought he had really gone off the deep end," David confesses. "I hurried to the lady's house to rescue him. To my surprise the lady appeared to be sane, quiet, and pleasant."

David took his son home. Day after day David watched him. Something *had* happened. His son *was* different. No drugs. No strange behavior. A completely new attitude. David was dumbfounded. Apparently all the money he had spent had availed nothing. But one sincere little prayer to Jesus had wrought a miracle. David looked and looked at his son and wondered.

"The lady began to visit us," David recalls. "I listened as she explained the Bible, though not without conflict. My wife and I were practicing meditation at the time; I even played one of our meditation records for the lady. She politely listened, and then she talked about the Bible some more. My wife, a graduate of USC, had majored in psychology, and her intellect told her religion was just a crutch. But the lady continued to come and talk to us.

"About two weeks later alone in my home I prayed, not really expecting to be heard. 'Jesus,' I said, 'I am a sinner. Come into my heart and cleanse me of my sins.' The amazing thing was that after I had prayed, I knew it had happened. God had accepted me, forgiven me. The long, long search for inner peace and rest had come to an end at the feet of Jesus. About six weeks later my wife committed herself to Christ.

"What an upheaval! Inner peace and joy replaced frustration and restless searching. Our whole set of values was turned upside down. Now Christ became of supreme importance, and then the spiritual welfare of others. Money, success, prestige, pleasure, all slid to the bottom of the list. Life suddenly became very meaningful and wonder-full."

Today David's son, restored to full health, is employed, married, and has a healthy, happy son. David sold his lucrative real estate business which demanded so much time from him. Today he oversees a large apartment unit.

"In these units I have found my field of ministry," David says. "How many are distressed, torn by family conflicts, coming apart as persons! I take care of my business with my clients first, and then I talk to them about One who loves them, who can help. I tell how he helped me. Some listen. Some don't. And some have committed themselves to Christ."

Although a tragic crisis in his son's life caused David Rothschild earnestly to seek for a meaning in life, the questions had been there, in his heart, for a long time.

Why Do Questions Arise?

Why, we might ask, do questions arise at this time of life when, in a sense, we are at our prime, when our income is the highest, when we are seeing our children blossom into young adults, when we have advanced in our work?

One reason we begin to ask questions is because we find ourselves looking both forward and backward in life. Usually we look forward: it is normal to plan for a future. But when we reach the middle years, we see ahead, looming closer than we would like, aging, decay, and finally the grave. It is natural to shy away from this, and so we find ourselves beginning to do what we shall continue to do in increasing measure, looking back. As we look back over the life we have lived, almost unconsciously we begin to reevaluate.

10

For those with families questions come also because of the vacuum created when the children move out of the home. Up until the middle years raising and providing for our family probably has brought the most meaning to our life. Now the children are gone. What shall we live for? This question becomes especially acute for those whose children move to a distant city, and miles separate not only parents and children but grandparents and grandchildren. So it is natural that as we give less and less time to our families, we begin to examine our other interests to see if they are worthy of our time, effort, and resources.

What Makes Life Worthwhile?

Success is important. We strive to attain perfection in our sphere of work, in music, art, business, politics, sports, skills. If we are religious, we may have worked hard to become as good a person as possible. Much attention has been given to our own personal spiritual life as well as to works of charity. Seminars on self-development and self-actualization and small-group therapy meetings may have engaged us. Books on self-improvement and self-understanding have been read.

The search for wisdom captivates some. Life is spent in the pursuit of truth. Leakey developed thick calluses on his knees kneeling on East Africa's parched soil, trying to excavate from the earth the secrets of the beginnings of man. Though he felt Leakey's aim to be noble, the president of the country where Leakey pursued his research, President Julius Nyerere of Tanzania, East Africa, declared that spending one's life in study is a luxury only highly developed countries can afford. Speaking to his own people, President Nyerere declared that as long as we have the poor and less fortunate in the world, education never should be for the individual, to raise the status and increase the comfort and enjoyment of the individual. No, Nyerere declared, education should be training for service, in order that those less fortunate might be offered the opportunities we enjoy.

11

Many do give their lives in service and feel deeply rewarded. Others long for security and dedicate their lives to maintaining a dependable world where their children and grandchildren can live in peace. Others seek to establish a climate of decency and civility where each person respects the feelings, dignity, and the God-given rights of his neighbor. Some ardently crusade for reform and change. And many, in their search for that which satisfies, pursue pleasure and entertainment.

All of this is good. Life takes on wholesomeness and wholeness when all of these goals in varying degrees, direct our living. But the question before us is: Are these goals alone enough? Do any of these separately, or even all of them together, satisfy us completely? Viewed from the perspective of eternity, are they as meaningful and significant as we had thought they were?

John W. Rilling recounts the story of Saint Philip Neri talking with a student at a university one day. The student's ambitions were great, and his talents forecast a successful career. The saint asked the student about his studies and his plans for the future.

"Right now I am studying philosophy," the student replied, "but I hope to graduate next year."

"And then?" queried the saint.

"Then I shall go on to study civil law and win my degree as a doctor."

"And then?"

"Then I shall become a lawyer and begin my practise."

"And then?"

"Then I expect I shall marry and settle down. I hope to have a family and probably will inherit the estate of my father."

"And then?"

"Why then I suppose I shall be satisfied with the position I have won, and shall be respected by my fellow-citizens; and then like everybody else, shall grow old and die."

"And then?"

The young man hesitated. His lips began to quiver. Two little words, "And then?" hauled him up short and caused him to think and reevaluate his carefully laid plans for his life.

The Need for Re-evaluation

The man who has not given his allegiance to God may not find too much difficulty smothering the questions that arise in his heart and reassuring himself that his life has been and is worthwhile. He determines his own value scale.

For the Christian it is different. The Christian accepts God's value scale made clear in the Bible. But because it is so easy to get side-tracked and forget that which should be central in our lives, we need to pause from time to time to ask ourselves some questions: Are the goals we set earlier in life meaningful enough for us to give the second half of our lives to their continuing achievement? Or have we accomplished our goals? Do we need to set new ones? Or have we drifted from youthful idealism and settled for second best?

How to Re-evaluate Life Goals

The reflection and questioning can be done at retreats. The hour before or after Sunday worship can be utilized for this as a group venture. Or we can do it on our own.

"Life was becoming so confusing and meaningless for me," a business man said, "that I finally asked for a couple of days off. I drove out to a little rented cabin in the desert and there thought and prayed my way back to tranquility and purposefulness."

Questionnaires can be helpful as guide lines. The best examination of all goes on when we let God question us through his Word. The psalmist of old has put into words for us a prayer we can pray: "Search me, O God, and know my heart! Try me, and know my thoughts! And see if there be any wicked way in me, and lead me in the way everlasting!" (Psalm 139:23, 24.)

Hindrances to Self-examination

"It takes courage to look back over one's life and reevaluate," a successful business man said to me one day after we had been discussing the subject. Indeed it does. For one thing, we might see the need for change, and it always takes courage to change.

13

"What would you do," another man asked, "if you felt you'd messed up your life?"

"I suppose I'd feel bad," I answered. "But I don't think I'd want to waste too much time on tears. I'd try to be thankful that life has not been lived in vain if I have now discovered what is truly important. I'd thank God for the forgiveness he has for me and then move on from there."

But even after we understand that God stands ready to forgive and accept us, we might be crippled from acting because we know our limitations and the possibilities of failure. And we wonder, much as we might desire it, if life really can be different. The good news is that it can, as we grow in experiencing the truth the Apostle Paul declared: "When I am weak, then I am strong," and "I can do all things through Christ who strengthens me."

Never Too Late

If we will only let Christ take over our remaining years of life, he will make something beautiful of them. He is able to do this. He wants to do this. It is comforting also to remember that life is not only longevity. It also contains the qualities of breadth and depth and these often outweigh the influences of longevity. Jesus lived only 33 years.

So it is never too late, and we must never feel the remaining time is too short. Lived with God, the remaining years can become our best years.

Before you set new goals, evaluate the goals you already have:

1. Is the career I have chosen satisfying? If not, is there anything I can do about it?

2. If I had to flee this country and take only ten possessions with me, what ten would I take?

3. If I had $3000 to spend as I wished, how would I spend it?

4. What frustrates and tires me? What bores me?

5. If I could live life over, what would I do differently?

6. If I had control over my future, what would I like it to contain?

7. When I think over my present life, what are the best aspects of it?

8. What in my present life am I most unhappy about?

9. What are my present goals?

10. For whom have I set these goals?

Write down what has brought meaning to your life:

1.

2.

3.

As you consider your past goals (whether they have been conscious or unconscious goals), how would you rate them? (Check one.)

1. Very satisfying and rewarding
2. Satisfying, but I feel there must be something more
3. The type of goals most people have, so I should be satisfied
4. Not as important now as I thought they would be 20 years ago
5. Not worth all the hassle

Do not set new goals for yourself yet. That will come in a later chapter.

Charley Horses, Aching Bones, and Bay Windows

Middle age is a time when you stop taking your body for granted and start taking care of it instead.
—B. FRIED

If we are going to be able to fulfill the goals we set for our second half of life, we are going to need as good health as possible. Thus caring for our body takes on meaning, and we are motivated to make called-for changes.

What changes are called for?

1. *Stop self-diagnosing and pay attention to warning signals.* Many of us have been used to diagnosing our own ailments and prescribing for them. Now, however, if we are interested in assuring ourselves of good health the last half of our life, we better seek the help of those professionally trained.

Of course, the way we have already lived life will make a difference too. We can't mistreat our bodies and thumb our nose at biological laws and not expect to pay the price. If we ate rich foods in our 20s, we began to deposit cholesterol and triglyceride plaques in our blood vessels. By our 30s these plaques had streae through them; in our 40s atherosclerosis is evident, and "the blood hangs in the veins like silt."

But what's past is past. The best we can do is take care of our bodies from now on. So don't play doctor any more.

Some of us stubbornly refuse to consult a doctor because we grew up under magnificent parents and grandparents who cheerfully and stoically accepted aches and pains as part of the lot of sinful man. This training was unfortunate, because ignoring an ache won't make it go away. Pain often is man's kindest friend, alerting him to hidden trouble that will only become worse if ignored.

The danger is greater for us too because the body sends back more subdued alarms than it did before; therefore "minor" complaints may be minor only in the degree they are actually felt. Take the matter of body temperature. In a child a temperature may soar to 104°, 105°; in a young person, 102°, 103°; in an older person it might not go higher than 100° or 101°, and yet the infection may be as great or even greater. But because we are conditioned to thinking in terms of the temperature of children, we pooh-pooh lower temperatures and refuse to regard them as serious.

We need to understand also that remissions usually do not occur spontaneously. Disorders that are ignored do not disappear but usually get progressively worse. So when the warning bell of aches and pains begin to ring, check in with your doctor.

2. *Follow your doctor's orders.* Many of us also have been inconsistent about actually following doctor's orders. We listen. If the diet recommended has seemed too hunger-causing, if exercise is too difficult to fit into an already over-crowded schedule, if the pills prescribed don't seem to "be doing any good," we often simply ignore the doctor's orders. Or we may obey doctor's orders for a while, feel better, and then, because we do feel better, fail to follow through on our doctor's recommendations.

Again, we need to understand that effective control treatment requires (1) diagnosis of the disease early enough before irreparable damage has occurred, and (2) continuing close cooperation.

You cannot treat disorders for a little while and then forget all about them just because the subjective symptoms have subsided, any more than you can navigate a ship by setting it upon a compass course and then ignoring it.

Change in attitude and response to warning signals is also important because the progression of many diseases may be arrested: high blood pressure, gout, pernicious anemia, diabetes,

18

thyroid inadequacy, even heart trouble. But we must assume responsibility for our own care. Only *we* can do it. Our physician should educate us and train us. Then we must take over.

We have in our congregation a sprightly, white-haired, pink-cheeked smiling man in his 70s, who has survived 25 years since his heart attack in middle age because he learned what restrictions to make and accepted them.

Mel Iverson's heart problems crept up on him slowly. When he was 53 he noticed his arms ached when he washed the car. They ached when he mowed the lawn. One day his wife came home and found him resting after every swath he cut. Lydia called the doctor. The doctor told her it was Mel's heart, but it wasn't serious. Shortly afterwards Mel was sitting in his office when he felt heavy pressure in his chest. He walked across the street to his doctor's office, but couldn't see the doctor because he had other patients. Mel went back to his office, and the pains increased. When he finally was able to see his doctor, he had already had an attack. For six weeks he rested in the hospital, waiting for nature to repair some of the damage.

Since that time Mel has had to exercise constant vigilance. He carries nitroglycerine tablets. Usually he takes only one a day, sometimes none, but during bad days he might have to take three. Whenever any exertion causes the slightest bit of pain, he stops immediately, takes a pill, and lies down to rest. When I talked with him recently, he had been trying to pull a few weeds, but his heart was protesting, so he had given it up for the day. On good days he can walk two miles, on bad days he might not be able to walk two blocks. He swims, but can't go in water deeper than five feet. "I don't like to wade with the kids," he confesses, "but I have no choice." He has learned to accept his limitations and adapt. This allowed him to work 12 years after his heart attack until his retirement at 65, and he continues an active life even now.

So serious health problems in the middle years need not mean a life of inactivity or invalidism. It often does mean a life where activities are curtailed to match the functional capacity of the body. And it is not always a question of being prohibited from doing certain things we might wish to do, but a question of how we do them.

3. *Proper care of our bodies now may help insure healthful years to come.* Change in our attitude toward the care of our bodies is important also because the care we give our bodies during our middle years can positively affect what our health will be like in our 60s and 70s. If we can reach 60 without one or more of the progressive disorders of old age, the outlook for the senior half of our second 40 years is hopeful indeed. If the chronic progressive disorders are discovered early, there is plenty of time for treatment to accomplish much. The early case of high blood pressure, arthritis, or hardening of the arteries may be of no immediate concern. Nor is a person likely to be disabled for a long time. Progression of disease can be slowed down if we are alert and obedient.

To maintain good health it is helpful for us to become informed about the most common ailments of aging and be able to recognize the early warning signals and know what to do about it.

Cardiac Problems

Doctors warn that if the person in middle years wants to avoid cardiac problems, he might have to make some changes if he is (1) a smoker, (2) overweight, (3) gets little exercise, (4) lives and works under a great deal of tension. Doctors agree that these are the four chief contributing factors towards making a person a likely candidate for heart problems of one kind or another.

George Rifa of Los Angeles had smoked for 35 years and had tried to stop for 10. At 46 George met Christ, and his whole life, which he had succeeded quite well in messing up, was revolutionized. The slavery to smoking, however, continued for another two years. Suddenly one day in church a word was spoken that struck him as a direct message from God that the day of liberation for him had come. He walked out of church and hasn't smoked since. For George it was a miracle. For others, dramatic miracles don't seem to happen. But then maybe we don't emphasize enough Christ's power to liberate.

20

Fighting overweight has been a life-long problem for me, demanding constant vigilance and discipline. I can remember sitting in the doctor's office when I was 18 and hearing the doctor say: "You might as well make up your mind right now that you're never going to be able to eat as much as most other people without putting on weight." At 18 I wasn't ready to accept that pronouncement. Midway through life I know he was right.

It's not easy to remain thin in this prosperous country of ours. Magazines, TV, radio, restaurants, and supermarkets all seem leagued in an all-out effort to make us fat. We have to learn to make faces at them.

A few lessons I have learned may help someone else.

1. I had to stop berating and tearing myself down. If I didn't have a body like a model's, what other God-given gifts did I have which I could develop? If I gained weight, rather than hating myself for it, I learned to say, "Oh-oh! time to take things in hand again." The quicker I took off the excess pounds the easier it was. I learned never to say, "I gained only two pounds this last year; I don't worry about that." Multiply two by twenty and what do I have? A fatty. My kidneys and heart and liver have remained the same size, but now they have to do the work for a body-and-a-half. And, oh, my poor aching legs and back! An overweight of 25% above normal increases 174% my chances of dying early, and only 10% overweight ups my chance of an early death 20%—and I love to live.

2. I had to stop blaming others—and God—for my being fat and accept responsibility for it myself. I grew up on a farm. Farmers work hard and burn up a lot of calories. Mother was a superb cook, and I just didn't realize I didn't need all the food my brothers ate. Habit patterns were laid early. I had to learn I could choose to change. If I was fat, I was the only one making me fat. And if I was to take seriously Paul's admonition in Romans 12 to present my body to God as a sacrifice, I better do the best I could to make it as *fine* a gift as possible, not as *big* a gift as possible.

3. I had to accept the fact that I never would be able to have, for example, all the ice cream I liked. But lots of people have

diet restrictions, so there was only one way to treat self pity: kick it out.

4. I often got hungry about 4 P.M. Having an apple or a skim milk strawberry or pineapple milk shake has helped ease me over that critical period. Being out of the house would help too, but I can't if I am going to prepare dinner for my family. Crispy cold celery or carrot sticks on the counter help take care of the snacking habit as I prepare dinner. If you chew gum, chew gum. You can't both chew gum and eat.

5. I am thankful for housework which provides some exercise, and I try not to be too efficient, so I walk more. I know better than to indulge in a calorie-laden pie thinking I'll walk it off later. As I understand it, I'd have to walk 40 miles to walk off a pound of weight!

6. When my will power gets really weak, I join a group that will counsel, encourage, and if need be, yank me up. It helps.

7. I am trying to cultivate new cooking habits. I'm experimenting with vegetables I hadn't used before. I broil, grill, or bake. We use non-fat milk. I limit beef to twice a week and include veal, fish, liver, and poultry. Fruit often provides the dessert. And I don't spend time drooling over tantalizing pictures of delectable goodies or reading their recipes.

8. When I'm taking off pounds that have crept on, I try to be patient. Even losing only one or two pounds a week adds up.

So much for weight loss to help us control our heart problems. The subject of coping with tension we'll consider in another chapter.

Cancer

Let us turn now to another disease we fear almost as much as heart trouble: cancer. Nearly 1/3 of the 350,000 Americans who die of cancer could be cured if the disease is diagnosed and treated in early stages. We need to be on the alert constantly for cancer's warning signals:

- A change in bowel or bladder habits
- A sore that does not heal

- Unusual bleeding or discharge
- Thickening or lump in the breast or elsewhere
- Indigestion or difficulty in swallowing
- Obvious change in a wart or a mole
- A nagging cough or hoarseness
- Unintentional loss of weight

If you notice any one of these, report to your doctor *at once*.

The Pap smear should be routine for women. Both men and women should ask for a proctoscopy when they have their yearly physical exam, to check for cancer of the colon.

Arthritis

Sooner or later, if you live long enough, you're going to be troubled with arthritis. According to the Arthritis Foundation "the patient with the beginning of arthritis who finds the right doctor early before irreversible damage to joints has taken place can expect to be saved from the serious effects of the disease."

Used now are (1) medications, to alleviate symptoms and pain; (2) exercise, posture correction, and physical therapy to prevent or postpone disablement; (3) surgery to rebuild, replace or prevent damaged joints.

The Arthritis Foundation, G.P.O. Box 2525, N.Y., 10001, has helpful pamphlets available free if you only write for them: *Rheumatoid Arthritis, a Handbook for Patients; Osteoarthritis, a Handbook for Patients; Home Care Program in Arthritis, a Manual for Patients; The Truth about Aspirin for Arthritis; The Truth about Diet and Arthritis; Arthritis—the Basic Facts.*

Alcoholism

An affliction which cripples to an even greater degree than arthritis because it attacks the spirit and soul of a person is alcoholism. Alcoholism becomes a special concern for us parents in our middle years, not only because of what it may be doing to us personally, but also because our example may be leading our children into a trap more vicious even than drug addiction.

Values are learned as our children see them modeled every day in every way. Are we trying to have double standards—one for ourselves, and one for our children?

Statistics have long told us alcoholism is a problem for many in the middle years. Alcoholism climbs a steep 50% in the 40–60 age group over the number of alcoholics in their 30s. One of the reasons for this is it usually takes from 15 to 20 years for a social drinker to get hooked and become an alcoholic. The middle-aged alcoholics come, not from Skid Row, but from business offices, from dental and doctors and lawyers' offices, from ministers' studies, from industry. Ninety-five percent of the alcoholics of our nation live and move in the stream of society. Of any random group at a large public gathering, 5 to 10% will be alcoholics, or every tenth person you see. Only mental illness and cardio-vascular disease are more prevalent among Americans. The danger is great because social drinking is so acceptable in our society.

Dr. Marvin A. Block, former chairman of the AMA Committee on Alcoholism, warns: "The bald fact is that any drinker, whoever he is, runs the risk of becoming an alcoholic, and many people in all walks of life are running the risk and losing. This doesn't mean that this consequence is inevitable in the case of every drinker, but the possibility is always there. This is the first thing that must be recognized by anyone who drinks. To complicate matters, one of the first effects of alcohol is the modifying of judgment. This makes of a drinker himself, a poor judge of whether or not he is drinking excessively. He, as a matter of fact, will usually be the last person of his family to recognize his changing manner of drinking."

Dr. Block has a questionnaire he asks his patients to fill out in an endeavor to uncover hidden cases of beginning alcoholism. He graciously granted me permission to reprint those questions here.

1. Is the desire for a drink of frequent occurrence, with emphasis on the *desire?*

2. Is there need for a drink at certain times of the day with emphasis here on *need?*

24

3. Is there anticipation of drinking in the evening, as the day wears on?

4. Is alcohol used to help sleep?

5. Does frequent drinking go beyond ritual socializing?

6. Is there a desire to get "high" and thereafter to maintain that plateau through more drinking?

7. Is there disappointment when drinks are not served at a restaurant or a private party?

8. Is there criticism of one's drinking by someone or anyone who cares?

9. Is there resort to a drink or more when there is discomfort of any kind, as a means of relief from tension, or from physical or psychological malaise?

10. Is care always taken to have a supply of alcohol on hand "just in case" or is there more than slight preoccupation with the consideration?

Dr. Block emphasizes that all who drink should constantly review their drinking patterns. If change and discipline are needed, change must be made.

Because the alcoholic usually is unwilling or unable to detect alcoholism in himself, others need to be on the alert for him. Warning signs at work are lower productivity, an increase in job errors or accidents, a more spasmodic work pace, excessive absenteeism or tardiness, unexplained temporary absences from the work place and leaving work early, frequent Monday absences, irritability and fatigue, worsening of relationships with others.

Dr. Jackson A. Smith of the Stritch School of Medicine, Chicago, describes the "social alcoholic." "He may have a routine martini at lunch, a couple more drinks before boarding the commuter train and again before dinner. There may be wine with dinner, but the drinking ceases with the meal. After dinner he will sleep soundly in his chair, then awaken to go to bed."

The biggest difficulty is motivating the alcoholic to seek help. If his employer is sympathetic, you can work through him. He has the power, through threat of firing or demotion, to intervene.

Neither logic or tears will move a person as much as fear of losing his job.

Rehabilitation centers to help the alcoholic and his family can be found in almost every city. I spent a few days visiting Hazelden in Center City, Minnesota. Hazelden combines a peaceful, rural setting with a homelike atmosphere. Skilled and compassionate professional staff give unstintingly of themselves, and because of their sacrificial service, the fees at Hazelden are within the reach of almost all. In addition, Hazelden can be justly proud of its record of 65% rehabilitation. But there are many other centers besides Hazelden that stand ready to help the alcoholic. Just turn to the yellow pages of your phone directory. Or ask your doctor or pastor.

Drug Addiction

Closely related to alcoholism is drug addiction, the creeping menace among middle-aged suburbanites. A young man we know is an apprentice in laying carpets in apartment units. "We have to work fast," he explained. "One of our men is middle-aged. To maintain the fast pace he keeps dropping pills down his throat. Really," the young man shook his head, "is that the way life has to be?"

Yet the practice has become so prevalent that Dr. Lawrence Smith, a general practitioner from the Los Angeles area, declares the suburban black-market trade in pep pills may become as lucrative as sales to youth. Women use them to elevate moods, to fight loneliness, and withstand the daily grind. And Dr. Harold Arlen of Santa Monica Hospital Medical Center says doctors prescribe more tranquilizers and barbiturates than any other medicines, with antibiotics coming in a poor second. At least some of these drugs can be classified as addictive, and constant users of them can be considered belonging to the drug culture. Middle-aged people need as much help fighting addiction to drugs as our young people.

For Women: Menopause

Surprisingly, many are ignorant of the most basic facts about menopause. Menopause means simply the final end of monthly menstruation, the end of a woman's child-bearing period. And that is about all it means. A woman remains a woman.

The average age of the menopausal woman is 47. The earlier a girl begins to menstruate, the longer she will continue. Pregnancies are unusual after 45, but they do happen, so women using contraceptives should continue to use them. How does a woman know she is approaching menopause? When a woman's periods become irregular or the amount of flow decreases, she is approaching menopause.

Some of the unpleasant symptoms which might be experienced are depression, sleeplessness, a racing or jerking of the heart, dizziness, frequent and difficult-to-control urination, vaginal dryness or itching, headache, numbness or tingling of fingers or toes, vague aches and pains, and an increase or decrease in sexual desire. Hot flashes are perhaps the most uncomfortable symptom.

Doctors estimate only 10% suffer acute discomfort and 20% have moderate symptoms. For most women no drugs are needed, just an understanding of what is going on. For those who are acutely uncomfortable, doctors can offer help through medications. Sometimes treatment not only relieves the distressing symptoms but also brings a measure of well-being and good health that a woman may not have known for years. And most important of all is the loving, understanding support of a husband who is sensitive and patient, and who leads the children into a kind caring role toward their mother.

For Men: the Mid-life Crisis

Is there a male menopause? There is, some declare. Nonsense, others protest. How could there be? A matter of semantics, others say. Call it the *climacterium* which Webster defines as "the bodily and psychic involutional changes accompanying the transition from middle age to old age," some advise. Some declare it is socio-cultural, that the Navajo Indians, for example, never experience it because they step into a new hierarchy at 45. They become leaders and give orders and advice, but do not have to perform.

Some say it is psychological. Others say the hormone factor enters in. Daniel J. Levinson, a Yale scientist and psychologist, who with five other team members has engaged in an intensive four-year study of the mid-life crisis of 40 men, defines the different developmental stages an adult man passes through in this way:

(1) Early twenties: "getting into the adult world." The young man is living independently of his parents, but still has not settled what he will do with his life. Friendship with an older experienced man who encourages, helps, and influences him is common in this era.

(2) Early thirties: "settling down." Establishing a home is prominent.

(3) From 36–Mid-forties: "becoming one's own man." The man now might chafe under authority and the restraints others place on him. This is the time in life when man wants most to know he has succeeded.

(4) Mid-forties–50: "mid-life crisis." The time of questioning and reevaluation, struggling to accept the disparity between his dreams and what actually has been accomplished, and asking if it is all worth it.

Symptoms of mid-life crisis have been described as nervousness, decrease of sexual potential, depressions, decreased memory and concentration, fatigue, disturbed sleep, irritability, loss of interest and self-confidence, indecisiveness, numbness and tingling, fear of impending danger, excitability and sometimes, though rather infrequently, headaches, vertigo, constipation, itching, sweating, and even tears.

A loving, loyal wife who is alert to what is happening to her husband, who understands and who will quietly support and care, can perhaps do more than anyone else. "This too will pass."

28

If the man is aware of what is going on, he can emerge stronger and more purposeful than ever.

Depression

Depression weighs heavily on the lives of millions. In this chapter we cannot begin to discuss it adequately, but it is so common we cannot ignore it entirely.

Depression varies in intensity from just being "in the dumps" to agony because one feels he is so completely different from everyone else. Nobody knows why, but most depressions wear out, many within weeks or months, the average being 18 months.

One aspect of depression that is not often understood is the rhythm of "highs" and "lows," or the balance that must take place between excitement and depression. Every excitement must be followed by a period of depression, which often corresponds in degree of intensity and length of duration with the preceding excitement. A fact which is even less understood is that not only mental excitements but even physical accidents involving physical injury and pain can cause an initial excitement which is followed by depression later on. Knowing this we can better understand those experiences in which a person who has been injured or bereaved is at first in such an exalted state that he seems oblivious of pain. But just as surely, depression must follow. Depression is nature's way of getting us to cut back and slow down so our motor will not burn out.

When we understand that depression is God's gift to us to keep us in balance, we won't have to go looking for or chasing the devil every time we get down in the dumps. He hasn't brought it on. A normal, chemical reaction in our body has triggered it into being for our own good, to protect and save us. It is true the devil lurks around when we are depressed, because we are vulnerable then, but we don't need to blame every depression on his direct action. Nor do we have to wonder if depression is the result of some sin we have committed. The depression is God's gracious gift to us; his warning signal to slow down. We need to receive it as such, with gratitude, take the cue and get needed rest or turn to some completely different activity which will relieve and refresh us.

When, however, depression persists month after month, for no specific reason (it is natural to feel depressed after one is bereaved or weak after a long illness), it's a good idea to have a talk with your doctor. This is especially true if you begin to feel everybody "has it in for you" or that your situation is absolutely hopeless. Or if you feel yourself becoming more and more tired every week or full of mysterious aches and pains for which your doctor assures you there is no physical cause, tell him you just do not feel well and ask him what he can recommend. A good physician will direct you to someone who understands how you feel and who can help you.

A Few Simple Rules

To further help us to maintain health in the middle years, here are a few simple rules to follow:

1. *If you are worried about something, check it out.* Examination, if nothing else, can alleviate fear, even when the examination uncovers a disorder. When a situation is thoroughly understood and when there is something we can do about it, it is not as fearful. A positive outlook on life contributes to good health, so get rid of fears.

2. *Get reasonable exercise, but get it regularly.* Most doctors agree swimming and walking are excellent. "A five minute walk," says Dr. Paul Dudley White, the eminent heart specialist, "will do more good to an unhappy, healthy adult than all the psychology and medicine in the world."

3. *Don't overlook the importance of adequate rest.* Adequate rest is important to avoid constant fatigue. With fatigue comes loss of zest. With loss of zest comes loss of interest in life.

Many people find as they move along through life they sleep less. But though they sleep less, they need more rest, more time to recuperate. If you can get them, short periods of rest throughout the day are immensely refreshing. It is well known that

Thomas Edison claimed he slept only four hours every night, but he was cat-napping all the time.

By our middle years we have become so accustomed to the accelerated pace of life that we find it hard to admit we need to change, we need to slow down. If you feel tired, don't fight the feeling. There's nothing sinful about a little "sanctified sloth," when it means taking care of our bodies. Incidentally, I've discovered a 5 or 10 minute rest is an excellent substitute for food, especially in the late afternoon. And short vacations and days "away from it all" recharge the body's "batteries."

4. *Give attention to good grooming.* How we look affects how we feel. Watch your posture. Make a conscious effort to straighten up.

5. *If you fall ill, allow more time for recovery than you did.* The older one becomes, the longer it takes the body to recover.

6. *Don't resent and fight against restrictions.*

7. *Have a good yearly physical exam.* Insist on thoroughness. My friend, Mary, had been having sporadic bleeding. Pap smears were negative. The bleeding persisted. Menopause was blamed for it. But Mary is a nurse, and the bleeding troubled her. Finally she insisted on a biopsy of tissue, and cancer was discovered. So, if you have doubts, be insistent on further exams, even at the risk of being told "it's all in your mind." The old adage is still true: "Better safe than sorry."

8. *Don't count on miracles.* People are healed through prayer, but this does not mean you should not explore and use every medical and surgical solution to your problem.

Having done all we can to care for our health, it's still possible that some of us will find ourselves suffering from some ailment that isn't going to go away. What do you do then? We'll consider that in the next chapter.

To Think About

What concerns you most now about your health?
What can you do about it?

3

When the Problem Doesn't Go Away

> *Patience. The ability to take a tragedy and turn it into a glory.*
>
> —WILLIAM BARCLAY

Christmas, 1966, in her missionary home on Mount Kilimanjaro Anna Vegdahl sat reading a book. Suddenly the words began to jog.

The next day and every day after that the words jogged. May came. Anna's eyes were still troubling her. She closed her left eye speculatively. She could read nothing with her right eye. It can't be, she thought. I'll go to bed. Maybe in the morning I'll find it's only a dream.

"I claim not to be emotional," Anna says, "but that night I wept. Questions buzzed around me like mosquitoes. Why had this happened? How could I believe God was in this? Was there any hope? What if I lost sight in my other eye? It was a long night, and by morning I still could not see with my right eye."

Anna went to Nairobi, Kenya, for examinations. The doctor thought it was only a hemorrhage that would clear up.

November 23, 1967, she left Tanzania on furlough. An examination by an eye doctor after she returned to the States reported lack of vision serious enough to prevent her return to Africa.

In January Anna noticed when she rode on a bus that all the houses she passed stood at an angle. Strangely enough, people seemed to be leaning over backwards. At church when she looked in the direction of the pulpit she saw only a pile of—what was it? Clouds? Rocks? But when she turned her head and stared at the side wall, out of the corner of her eye she could make out the outline of a man in the pulpit. "I felt self-conscious about sitting this way in church," Anna said. "I was sure I looked dumb sitting there staring at a wall."

Anna went to a specialist. He looked and looked in her eyes, then called in another specialist who looked and looked. They called in a third who also looked and looked. Then the three retired to a conference room where Anna could hear the low murmur of their voices. In the end they told her to come back in a month and sent her home with some tablets.

Well, Anna thought, *if I'm not going back to Africa, I better find a teaching position.* But when principals learned she had visual difficulties, they had no openings. Besides she was too old and too well trained.

Mission procedure required her to resign. For every five years of service overseas she was to receive two months' salary. March 31st she received her last check from the Board of World Missions. She sat in her apartment and stared out the window. Only dimly could she make out the outline of the building across the street. Bleakly she realized her left eye too had deteriorated.

"Suddenly," Anna confesses, "I began to feel sorry for myself. No more checks. Savings almost nil. Maybe going to Africa had been a mistake after all. If I had stayed home, I would have received a much higher salary and saved some and I wouldn't have forfeited my teacher's retirement which I had cashed in when I went to Africa.

"I jerked myself up. It was wrong of me to think this way! Hadn't it been clear to me I should go? Hadn't God promised his grace would be sufficient?

"I tried to count my blessings: my family, friends, the fact I had some sight, that I had had many good years and had received a good education. But past blessings don't pay today's rent."

Despair plagued Anna the following weeks. She began to lock her door so she could wash her face and powder her red nose before she let unexpected guests in. By April the doctor pronounced Anna legally blind, that is, her peripheral vision, which remained, was not enough to enable her to work. She went home and wept. Friends gathered, laid hands on her, and prayed. Nothing happened except that briefly she felt touched and comforted by God's presence.

Hope came when some fellow missionaries stopped in for a visit. "Surely you qualify for disability insurance from the board," they said. Anna had not been aware of this provision. She contacted the board.

The board had not realized the extent of Anna's trouble. In her concern not to be a burden to anyone, Anna had hesitated to tell things as they were. Also, when you look at Anna she does not appear blind, as her peripheral vision enables her to get around on her own. When the board understood the situation, they put Anna back on the payroll immediately and began to search for further ways to help her.

"I felt better right away," Anna says. "I began to believe things might work out after all."

She registered with the Services for the Blind, and received a record player. She ordered records of the New Testament. Friends came and took her out. Anna no longer felt the need to lock her door.

Preparing Ourselves to Adjust to Afflictions

Statistics tell us only 3% of those in the middle years are disabled by chronic disease like Anna was. Only one out of seven men and one of every eight women are limited to some degree. But after sixty-five, even though only 15% are disabled, 50% have to live with limitations of varying degrees. So knowing what lies ahead for us, we can use the middle years to cultivate and make habitual those attitudes which will help us bear the physical disabilities and pain sure to come, and bear them in such a way that life for ourselves and those around us will be, not only liveable, but full of cheer.

Three arthritic pain-filled decades have afforded Dorothy Trued of Detroit, Michigan, ample opportunities to learn.

"Each stage of attrition has been a battlefield of the spirit as well as the body," Dorothy confesses.

"I am grateful," Dorothy says, "for an otherwise strong body which has enabled me to continue the use of strong medicines over a long period of time. I am thankful too that I have always been an optimist. Life is no joke to me, but I feel its pleasing and joyful sides find too little expression among many. So mine is almost a compulsion to brighten somber faces.

"I am grateful too that my husband, Con, has been the kind of helper he is and able to care for me. Together we have fought against a relentless enemy, planning strategy and sharing our defences. And our congregation! No persons could have had finer Christian friends to support and encourage."

Dorothy admits that an increasing problem is the good will of people who try to assist her. Even a gentle squeeze can be painful. A child falling on her leg can leave a painful bruise for weeks. So she finds herself caught between wanting to be with people and being afraid of them simultaneously. "Emotions become very taut at times," she confesses. But her husband hastens to reaffirm her victories in this struggle. "Wherever Dorothy goes," he says, "she radiates a warmth and interest and an outgoing concern for others that never ceases to surprise or impress me."

Understandably, in the privacy of her home, Dorothy occasionally gives way to depression. The frustration of decreasing capability sometimes drives her into brief sessions of rage and bitterness. "I need more faith and patience to cope with such moods," Dorothy says. "I have no question about God's presence and care, although I have wondered about his involvement in my physical illness. Prayer is essential to my life although no unique ways of prayer have been tried by me. I am open to God's healing grace. I would never be critical of those who seek health through faith healing, and I am grateful when friends receive benefits. But for me to make special spiritual efforts to 'persuade God' to heal me is not consistent with my attitude of an all-knowing, caring God who knows my needs before I ask him. At some point, it seems to me, I must accept illness and death as something unconquerable, besides being incomprehensible. So I do not feel that if I am not healed, I am either lacking in faith or weak in some spiritual technique. I accept instead God's answer to Paul: 'My grace is sufficient for you.'

"Hope is one of the consolations of an arthritic," Dorothy says. She keeps wondering when some medical discovery will be made which will control or cure her illness. "Hope is a powerful sustainer of life," Dorothy declares. "Few people, I feel, know that better than I do."

An Aid to Fruitful Service

Sometimes a disabling illness does not imprison one to a chair or bed. Then a stout, stubborn spirit can enable one to carry on with one's work. Drowning out the pain by intense absorption in something else can even cause one to produce more than would otherwise be possible. This has been true for Lloyd Burke, pastor of Angelica Lutheran Church in downtown Los Angeles.

Pastor Burke was only 38 years old when arthritis began to plague him. He was living in Oakland at the time. The day he felt it in his shoulder he thought it was only a strained muscle. *Probably happened when I helped E. G. push his stalled car,* he thought. *Oh well, it'll go away.*

The pain didn't go away. Instead it ran around to the other shoulder and up his neck. It chased down his spine and halfway down knotted up into what felt like a billiard ball when he lay on his back.

"Probably bursitis," the doctor said, and gave him medication.

A call came to leave his parish in Oakland and venture out in a new project, the opening of Christ the King church to be housed in an office building in the heart of Chicago. Burke accepted the call.

Commuting to work gobbled up two precious hours a day. Because the downtown venture was an experiment, attention focused on it. Then the news media discovered it. Church people voiced reservations and doubts. Burke was on the spot. Could he produce? With no previous program or pattern to follow, temptations to inadequacy began to plague Burke.

As the months passed, and as voiced criticism grew in crescendo—or equally as devastating, when the venture was ignored and treated simply as if it wasn't there—Burke felt the billiard ball in the middle of his back growing bigger and bigger, and the gnawing pain in his shoulders and neck became his constant companion.

Exploratory surgery confirmed the doctors' diagnosis: arthritis. The prognosis: it'll get worse. The treatment: pills and shots. The advice: learn to live with it.

Relax, the doctors said. How can I, Burke argued, when I spend five, six hours a day listening to peoples' troubles? And how can you relax when you're in pain?

"Take time out for recreation," the doctors ordered.

"The only recreation I have time for," Burke answered, "is showing guests the city."

"Find a less demanding job," the doctors suggested.

"I felt God was leading me here," Burke replied. "I really have no choice then, do I? Could I be happy elsewhere?"

Looking back now Burke admits if he had understood more clearly the relationship between tensions and illness, and what can be done to alleviate tension, he probably could have prevented his arthritic condition from becoming as bad as it did. As it was, he plunged deeper and deeper into the work. Pain was new to him. He lashed out at it, angry that it had taken captive his body. But the pain only worsened, and began to pull his head down between his shoulders, giving him a hunched-over appearance.

Six and a half years passed. Then Burke accepted a call to Angelica, in Los Angeles. A historic and beautiful church, in the early days Angelica was surrounded by stately palms and elegant spacious residences and bathed by a warm southern California sun. But like almost all other cities across the land, the heart of Los Angeles too began to decay. As crowded conditions and congestion took over, people began the migration to the suburbs.

And the old Swedish Lutheran Church struggled to understand how it could effectively minister where it was.

Burke plunged into the work. The exhausting pain persisted and drove him to seek the help of a renowned doctor, famed for his skill in caring for arthritic patients. The doctor's diagnosis and prognosis were the same as before: arthritis—it will get worse.

"I suppose," Burke said with a wry smile, "that I'll have to learn to live with it."

The hulking big doctor, who faced him from across the desk, studied him. "No," he said slowly.

"No?" Burke leaned forward stiffly, eagerness tinging his voice.

"No," the doctor said, making a little tepee with his fingers, "No. You must learn to live *above* it. You must keep busy. If you concentrate on your work, become absorbed in it, you'll learn to transcend your pain. You'll be able to endure it until you get home at night and pick up the paper."

So again he plunged into work. *The wider my interests,* he reasoned, *the more I'll have to think about.* So almost every call to service was greeted by "Yes!" from him. Seminary, church finance board, community services, hospital boards, radio and TV spot devotions, chaplaincies, teaching at 32 continuing education seminars for pastors, writing, searching for answers to the problems of the lonely aged who rot away in the inner city— wider and wider his interests spread.

He read. He thought. He prayed. When pain kept sleep at bay, Burke would abandon the bed and pad his way into his study to prepare sermons. So the long night hours would pass, and as the gray light of dawn began to creep into his study he would pad his way back to his bed, to ease himself, exhausted now, into bed. Sleep, blessed sleep, would wrap her arms about him. A couple of hours later he would awaken and for one blissful moment he would lie there without pain. Then he would move and there was the pain again. Pilgrim in *Pilgrim's Progress* laid down his burden, but always picked it up again. He could too.

Pastor Burke believes that the tension-ridden situation in Chicago definitely contributed to his arthritis becoming as severe as it has.

"If you could do it over," I asked, "would you do it differently?"

We were sitting in his elegantly panelled, spacious church office. Burke settled stiffly into his swivel chair, facing the open window, and slowly lit his pipe.

I repeated my question, "Would you seek out an easier situation where the tension would be less?"

He wheeled around. "No! No, of course not!"

"But the price you have paid is great."

"The satisfaction of sticking with a difficult situation was greater. I grew. I learned to accept difficulties as posts to build around. The whole situation challenged me to prove myself. It called forth courage to go ahead with what I felt was right, even where there was opposition. No, I never would have been ready for Los Angeles without Chicago. The difficulties there taught me to rely on my parishioners and my Lord for support. And the pain—the pain has disciplined me. I have to concentrate on my reading, my writing, my work, concentrate so hard I forget the pain.

"Besides," he tilted back his swivel chair, his head and neck rigid as though fenced in by splints, "as children of God, don't we have to remember who is our Lord and make our decisions accordingly? Then if the ministry is demanding to the point of pain-producing," he ran his hand inside his coat sleeve up the arm where earlier I had noticed the collapsed capillaries, "well, then," he said, "you ask yourself which is more important, to escape tension so you can live as long and painlessly as possible or to accept tension and let it lead you to a fuller life." He paused, then added, "I prefer the richer life."

As we review the stories of Anna, Dorothy, and Lloyd, we can note what attitudes have helped them so we can give attention daily to cultivating those attitudes. Oswald Chambers declared once that it is only as we practice in the daily humdrum situations of life that we shall be able to be victorious when the crisis comes. From the stories of Anna, Dorothy and Lloyd we also can note, as guidelines, courses of action to follow when problems don't go away.

Attitudes

1. Kick out self-pity.
2. Focus on what you *have*, not on what you do not have.
3. Acceptance of the mystery of pain will lead to trust.
4. Keep hope alive.
5. Learn to like and accept what you see in the mirror now. In the years to come you may like even less what you see, so you might as well learn to like yourself now.
6. Learn the art of compensation.
7. Cultivate a sense of humor.
8. Thank God for difficult situations. Received aright, they help us grow.

Courses of Action

1. Research your problem as thoroughly as possible.
2. Share your problem with friends. They may know about help that you are not acquainted with.
3. Take advantage of provisions that exist.
4. Continue circulating in society so you don't rust.
5. Learn how to cope with tension.
6. Concentrate on something or someone outside of you. Keep turning outwards.
7. At the same time, don't let your inner well go dry. Feed your inner life. Stay green.
8. When faced with decisions, the deciding factor is, not, what is there in it for me? but rather, what do I believe God wants me to do?

To cultivate the spirit of thankfulness which goes a long way in helping us bear the hard situations in life, here's a suggestion:

Get a notebook with at least 365 pages. At the top of each page put a date—January 1, January 2, etc. Then each day write down *one* thing that happened that day that brought happiness or made you thankful. At the end of 5 or ten years you will have in your Happiness Book a treasure money could never buy. As a bonus, you will have cultivated the habit of looking for that which brings joy. As you look, you'll discover many facets of happiness surrounding you of which you had not been aware of before. And yours will be a thankful spirit.

4

Coping with Tension

> *The world is too much with us, late and*
> *soon,*
> *Getting and spending, we lay waste our*
> *powers.*
> *Little we see in Nature that is ours,*
> *We have given our hearts away, a sordid*
> *boon.*
> —WILLIAM WORDSWORTH

"The pain in my neck has been getting worse. I even get short, jabbing pains down my arms now."

"Here?" asked the school district's doctor, her long, sensitive fingers searching for the trouble spot.

"I think the whiplash I got in a traffic accident three years ago must be causing the trouble."

"Three years ago? Where do you teach, Mrs. Rollins?"

"Hartford Elementary."

The doctor nodded. Hartford Elementary, she knew, was multiracial with blacks predominating. As the doctor continued her examination she encouraged her patient to talk.

"It was quite a challenge when they offered me the position as principal last year. I thought hard work and proper teaching would put things right.

"Yes?"

"We made progress too. But then I came back this fall and things were worse than ever." A sigh slipped out. Mrs. Rollins stiffened in her chair. "The thing that's hard to take," she burst out, "is that they're my people." From deep within a sob was wrenched out.

The doctor slid a white-coated arm around the woman's shoulders. "You're sure the pain in your neck is from the whiplash?"

"No," said the woman, throwing back her head, "no, it's from my disappointment in my people."

All of us feel the tightening effect of tension. Those in the middle years feel the pressure in a unique way.

Caught between two generations—our own adolescent or young adult children who probably don't understand us, and our aging parents who probably *still* don't understand us—we sometimes feel trapped. At work we may feel a slave to routine, or we may be edgy because of the competition we feel from the smart young ones moving up on us. Our schedule is crammed so full waking hours cannot possibly provide enough time to do all that "is on the list." Or old activities no longer attract; we are pulling back, and boredom is setting in with its own crabbiness-producing pressure. The world seems to be going to pot. New car doors stick or have drafty gaps. Young employees are irresponsible. Politics are "dirtier" than we had ever dreamed. Computers mess up monthly billings, and have you ever tried writing to a computer? Aches and pains warn us our bodies are decaying. Unemployment rudely jolts us. Too many of our friends are getting divorced or toppling over dead. Our aging parents are becoming senile, requiring care. Our mates, normally cheerful, are often depressed and cranky. Tension is everywhere.

Warning Signs That Tension Is Building Up

As the tensions build up, our bodies begin to cry out and protest. Blood pressure shoots up. Pulse rate quickens. The adrenal system is overworked. Indigestion, chronic tiredness, headaches, dizziness, vague pains, arthritis, hitherto unknown, now appear.

"See what anxiety and tension did to me," Mrs. Alice Wright, retired instructor of journalism from Long Beach City College, said to me, holding out her hands, knobby with arthritic bumps. "The last months as I watched my dear mother fail and die, I watched also the joints of my fingers swell and become dis-

44

torted." Mrs. Wright moved her fingers slowly as she talked. "After mother died, the swelling was arrested. It spread no farther."

How Can We Cope with Pressure and Tension?

We shall consider first some common sense approaches to the problem. Then we shall consider the special help available to us because we are Christians.

1. *Learn how to deal with frustrations and disappointments.* They make a hefty contribution to tension.

First, *avoid them if you can.* Often it is not the major crises of life that cause us to fall flat but rather the little daily annoyances: faucets that drip and drip, sliding closet doors that go off the track, closets over-full, habits of others that irritate us.

I find it helpful to write down what is constantly bugging me. Then I ask, Is there anything I can do about it?

In our home scissors and nail clippers never seemed to be in the drawer where they were supposed to be. When my husband began to complain that the only thing he could ever find to clip his nails were pinking shears, I knew it was time for action. I bought scissors and nail clippers for every room. It solved our problem. (Well, almost.)

The same principle applies to the larger, knottier problems we face. Can we do something about them? Then let's do it.

If problems defy solution, then we accept the situation, instead of fighting it.

In his letter to the Philippian Christians Paul declared: *"I have learned* in whatever state I am, to be content."

Again and again in the Old and New Testaments we can see how God worked in spite of, and sometimes *through,* disappointments and frustrations to bring about his purpose. Think, for example, of Moses' mother having to hide him in the bulrushes and Pharaoh's daughter finding him. Or of Joseph being sold by his brothers to the Egyptians. The Scriptures are full of examples.

We have to learn to accept the little daily annoyances too. Suppose it irritates you that your husband dumps all the screws, nails, ballpoint pen tops, and other paraphernalia of his pockets in the drawer with his neatly folded socks until the drawer looks like the aftermath of a Midwestern tornado. Well, chances are you're not going to change him, so why keep on trying and wearing both of you out? Accept it. Be glad the junk isn't dumped on the coffee table in the living room. Or in *your* drawer. After all, it's *his* drawer. And you can close it. Who else but you and he knows what it looks like anyway? Which leads to the next point.

Keep disappointments and frustrations in perspective. I remember once when mother was visiting us, and one of our children broke a cup I had prized. I was beginning to you-know-what when Mother said quietly, "It was only a cup." When I had cooled off a bit, she continued, "A cup can always be replaced,. And even if it can't, it was only a cup." In a flash I saw what I was doing to my child by my peevish scolding was infinitely more serious than the broken cup. It was, after all, only a cup, and an accident had broken it.

2. *If you are faced with a problem for which you see no solution, put it on the shelf for a while.*

My sister, who is left-handed, could find no one to teach her to knit. She struggled and tried and finally gave up in despair. One night she dreamed she was knitting. The next morning she got up, picked up her needles and clickety-clack away she went.

We discredit the power of our subconscious to go to work for us, especially with problem solving. Accept Christ's invitation to cast all your cares on him. In prayer commit to him the snarled problem. Drop it. Let it slip down into your subconscious. Turn your attention elsewhere. In due time the answer will pop up—fresh and right. I've had it happen many times.

3. *Turn interruptions and interferences into opportunities.* With today's busy pace of life and crowded schedules, interruptions and interferences often string us even tighter. But lest we think we are uniquely tested, turn to the Gospel accounts of the life of Jesus and notice all the times he was interrupted. Write "interruption" in the margin every time you find one. And then marvel. For Jesus constantly turned interruptions into opportunities.

46

A grandmother friend of mine in Los Angeles told how a granddaughter came home from a youth meeting at their church one night with three runaway youth in tow. Her mother—God bless her!—got out of bed and made up beds for the boys in the house trailer in the back yard. Then, handing the lads some of her husband's pajamas, she suggested they shower. While they did, she scooped up their clothes and tossed them in the washer. While the clothes tumbled dry, she fed the boys, and sent them to bed. The result of this mother's handling an interruption—and one that interrupted her night's sleep at that—in the right way was that one of the boys was reunited with his family back in the Midwest.

So when interruptions intercept, hang loose. Relax and look for the opportunity.

4. *Learn to pace yourself.* Try to understand how much you can do easily in a given length of time. Then don't over-program yourself. This in itself will ease some of the strain and help you cope better with interruptions. You'll probably find yourself getting more out of life too. For example, it's difficult to arrive breathless as the church doors are swinging shut and then be ready to really worship.

5. *Find someone with whom you can talk out your problems.* "I know I can always talk to God," you say, "and I try to turn to him. But sometimes I'd like to have a human ear listen to me, and they're hard to come by."

Well, if you don't have a friend who will listen, then you can begin by being a listening friend for someone else. The principle "give and it shall be given unto you" works in finding friends too.

"I'm hesitant to listen to other's troubles," you protest. "What if I don't have an answer?"

Maybe we don't have to have the answers! As our friend talks to us, quite possibly things will clarify for him, and he will arrive at new understanding.

Elisabeth Kübler-Ross, the Swiss psychiatrist who has ministered to hundreds of dying patients, says that when she first came to America the only place she could find employment was in the schizophrenic ward of a New York hospital. She soon discovered what she had learned in books was of little real help. So, not knowing what else to do, she listened to the patients. The result was 94% of the cases, formerly considered hopeless, were discharged. So great is the healing power of listening.

So find someone with whom you can talk out your problems, and the first step toward finding someone might be your listening to others first.

6. *Substitute cooperation with people for competition.* In Mark 9 we read about the disciples arguing with each other as to who is going to be the greatest in the kingdom. Jesus wisely remained silent and let them carry on. But that night, probably after supper, he quietly asked them, "What were you talking about today on the way?" Embarrassed, they fell silent and looked at each other. Then Jesus pointed out the superiority of cooperation over competition when he declared: "If any one would be first, he must be last of all and servant of all."

We see the spirit of competition popping up again in the early church when it would seem there was a contest on as to who could baptize the most, and the new Christians were chalking up scores for Apollos and Paul. Paul vigorously rebuked them and reminded them we are all part of one body. The finger should not compete with the nose, but rather cooperate with it and apply a handkerchief to it when it needs blowing!

But let's face it. Substituting cooperation for competition is difficult for Americans. America emphasizes the value of the individual. "How can *you* become a whole person?" How often we hear this emphasis.

When we emphasize the individual, we have competition. When we emphasize the community, we have cooperation. Competition sows seeds of distrust, envy, strife, tension, crooked play. Cooperation yields contentment, appreciation, an easing of burdens, encouragement, and affirmation even at times of setbacks.

Even husbands and wives can compete. And so can children in a home. Competition rears its ugly head in church work too. One aspect of our work overseas I appreciated was the fact that all missionaries were on the same salary scale. The only differences were in allowances made for the number of children in a

48

family and the number of years of service. Aside from that, the agricultural worker in the villages received as much as the medical doctor in the hospital. What would happen in this country if within our church pastors of 200-member churches received as much as those in larger churches or those in administrative positions?

7. *If possible, don't make too many changes at one time.*

Have you seen the social readjustment rating scale which Dr. Richard Rahe and Dr. Thomas Holmes drew up? In it they give point value to different changes we experience. Death of a spouse rates highest with 100, divorce follows with 73, personal injury accounts for 53, etc. If the total points add up to 150 or less, you have a 37 percent probability of being ill in the next two years. If the points total 155 to 299, your chances of becoming ill rise to 51 per cent; and if it zooms beyond 300 or more, the chances are 80 percent.

A friend of mine lost her daughter (estimated at a point value of 63). Her other daughter developed ulcers (45). Debts incurred because of her first daughter's lengthy illness accounted for 17 more points. A third daughter married (39), another daughter left home (29). My friend had gained weight so her doctor put her on a diet (15). She wasn't sleeping well because she was grieving for her daughter who had died (16). As is so often the case, she and her husband, feeling angry and resentful because their daughter had died, took their anger out on each other and began to quarrel (35). She was unable to respond sexually (39). For months before her daughter died, she had to care for her. Now she had to revise her personal habits and time schedule (25). Formerly they entertained often; now her husband became moody and withdrawn and wanted no one (15). The whole thing totaled to a whopping 338 points. In less than a year's time, cancer, which had plagued my friend 20 years earlier, flared up again.

8. *Make your vacations a time of complete change from your daily routine.*

Experiment with short vacations. A weekend, a day away from

home and work is beneficial. Even two, three hours can bring relaxation, refreshment and renewal.

9. *Learn to relax your muscles consciously.* Become aware of where you tighten up. Shoulders? Neck? Jaw? Eyebrows? Legs? Mouth?

Before one of our children was born I spent time each day going through exercises designed to teach me to relax. They must have been helpful. My baby was born in 20 minutes' time! I often still go through some of those exercises when I lie down, and usually I drop off to sleep within 5 or 10 minutes to awaken 5 minutes later, refreshed. Maybe we should instruct all our business and professional men in exercises to relax, not that they may have babies easily, but to help them reach retirement age without a heart attack.

10. *For the Christian, worship and directing our thoughts Godward offers perhaps the most significant solution of all in learning how to cope with tension.*

I asked Dr. Conrad Lund, President of the Lutheran Bible Institute of Seattle, how his Christian faith helps him cope with tension. I knew Dr. Lund lives with an overcrowded calendar, fractured schedules and commitment deadlines. The fact that the school receives its support chiefly through voluntary gifts adds its own peculiar tensions. I knew too that the prelude to an ulcer and a heart attack had alerted Pastor Lund to the toll tension has taken and that he was trying to learn how to cope with it.

Pastor Lund outlined four steps:

(1) *I must admit my need, my failure to manage on my own.*

The first signs of approaching defeat begin inside one's body. Blood pressure increases, the heart speeds its pace, muscles tense, and other vital signs signal the onset of an overload. Instead of concentrating on holding all of this in, unseen and unnoticed by even my wife and family, I concentrate on agreeing with God about the verdict life is placing before me. "God," I pray, "I cannot handle this. I need your forgiveness for the pride that makes me avoid you. I need your grace."

(2) *I set my mind on Christ, who is my life.*

I picture him in a similar situation. I see that he remains calm, at peace, content, sure of his Father's care, and of the grace of the eternal spirit, enabling him to offer himself in all things to God without blemish (Hebrews 9:14). I then affirm, "I cannot. But, God can."

(3) *I review the experiences I have had of God's grace operative and effectual in my life and also pertinent and powerful promises of Scripture that come to mind as applicable to my situation.*

Thus aided and encouraged, I affirm, "Since God can, I can. I am his, and with God all things are possible."

(4) *I thank God for any and all situations that come my way.*

Contentment then becomes a reality, even in the midst of still present distresses. The primary alteration by which all is made new is a change of view. I say, "My times are in God's hands," (Psalm 31:14), and then I rely upon the strength and the kindness of his hands. My life is committed to Jesus Christ. I want him to direct, to enable and to assign my life as it pleases him. That realization helps me to see incidents within accidents, opportunities within importunities, and appointments within disappointments.

As fellow learners with Pastor Lund, learning how to handle stress creatively could be one of the most important lessons we can learn during our bonus years. To a large extent it will determine how long we live and to what degree we shall be able to fulfill our goals. Learning to live with, use, and overcome tension is worth every effort we can make.

To Think About

As you have read this chapter have you become aware of areas of tension with which you need to deal? Do you see ways in which you may deal with them? If so, write them down.

5

Marriage — Sagging or Soaring?

> *All living relationships are in process of change, of expansion, and must perpetually be building themselves new forms.*
>
> —ANNE MORROW LINDBERGH

Lois couldn't believe her ears. Her husband, Roger, was standing by the side of her bed, holding out to her a cup of coffee. She thought she had heard him say "You'll be served divorce papers today," but how could she have heard that? Married 29 years and then divorce?

"Divorce?" she heard herself screaming. "Why?" And she shot out of bed.

She received no answer. Roger had already pushed his way past 19-year-old Gail standing in the doorway and disappeared.

Later, as Lois was speeding along the freeways on her way to work, she recalled Roger's business failures and the years of paying back debts. Roger had wanted so badly to be rich. She had tried to help him. And now this thanks for her loyalty! Hot tears blurred her vision. She took the wrong freeway turnoff but wasn't aware of it. We didn't ever really quarrel, she thought. Except over Gail. Gail was so outspoken. "Dad, I'd rather have fewer things and more stability. And see more of you." Roger always exploded when Gail started talking like that. He'd jump Gail. And then she, Lois, would defend Gail. And Roger would accuse her of loving Gail more than him. *I'm lost!* she thought, suddenly observing the street signs.

Three days later Roger returned home unexpectedly and stayed for three months. Lois outdid herself trying to please him, cooking his favorite foods, catering to his wishes, avoiding conflict. Then she discovered another woman was involved, a widow who sympathized with Roger and supported him in his feelings against Gail. Still Lois hoped things would work out.

A business trip took her out of the city three days. She returned to find Roger's closet and drawers empty. A note said, "I've been a failure as a husband and provider."

It was Friday. Lois went into the bathroom and just stood. All life's happenings flashed before her as though on a TV screen. She reached into the cupboard and took out a bottle of sleeping pills and started to pour them into her palm. Then her mind flicked on scenes of Gail with little children around her. She began to weep, and with shaking hands poured the pills back into the bottle.

Lois moved into a smaller apartment and set about to pay the bills her husband had run up on their credit cards. The middle of June she drove to the small simple cabin they had in the desert. There, alone, in the 105° heat, she cried, screamed, and yelled. She wrote letters and tore them up. She threw away her wedding ring. At last, exhausted and spent, she returned home.

The next week people at church found out what had happened. A friend took Lois to prayer therapy classes being conducted in their church for twelve weeks. In the little groups of eight Lois was asked, "Why are you here?" She broke down and wept.

The sharing, caring and praying together was a healing experience. One night Lois knelt by her chair. "Father," she sobbed. "I need you so! I want to turn my life over to you. I'm sorry I tried to get along on my own. Will you take me back?"

Of course, I will, God seemed to say. *Be patient, my child. Let me put the pieces in place.*

Awed, Lois arose from her knees. She went to bed, and for the first time for many months slept soundly.

In August, the day the divorce was finalized, Lois phoned Roger. He invited her for dinner. She went. Gently she tried to share with him what had happened to her. He listened and even let her pray. They continued to meet periodically and to talk and pray. A year later Roger said, "I'd like to remarry you." Lois wasn't sure.

"Can I come to church with you?" he asked.

Again Lois hesitated. Then, thinking, "If I refuse him, I haven't really forgiven him," she consented.

It was Communion Sunday. They knelt together at the rail, and Lois' eyes overflowed again. Later at the church door her pastor enveloped both her hands in his and said, "God bless your communion." Then he turned to Roger and bear-hugged him, while Lois unashamedly wept.

"You can't love two women at one time," Lois said to Roger later.

"I've broken with the other one," Roger said gently.

They continued to meet, to talk. They both read Eric Fromm's book, *The Art of Loving*. Insight into themselves came. They dated frequently, spent a weekend cleaning and painting their desert cabin, laughing and enjoying each other. They began to understand how play and humor recreate and replenish stores of human strength and self-respect. And always they talked and talked and read the Bible together and haltingly prayed.

In September Lois took a vacation. "I have to get away from you and put my head together," she told Roger.

Remarrying would involve forgiveness she realized. With God's help I can forgive, she thought. But there were other problems.

During their months of separation she suddenly had become an individual—with her own convictions. She had thought the trouble between them caused by Gail had been only father-daughter trouble. Now she was startled as she realized Gail had been vocalizing what she, Lois, had felt all these years. She too really would have been much happier with a steady job for Roger rather than all the risky business ventures. But in her desire to be a good and submissive wife, she hadn't said anything. *Why!* she realized now, *I wasn't being fair to him. I wasn't telling him how I really felt. We weren't working things out together. I had thought a good relationship meant absence of tension and conflict. I tried to repress my feelings and thoughts, not understanding that life is made up of alienation, forgiveness, and reconcilia-*

tions. But now it can never be the same again. Something has happened to me. I'm a different Lois, a Lois with convictions who will speak out, a Lois to whom God and the Bible and prayer and tithing are important. Will Roger accept the new Lois?

Yes, her heart told her. *Roger likes the new Lois. He's tried to tell you all summer.*

But what if I am hurt again? I can't stand the thought of being hurt again.

You have to take the risk, a little inner voice said. *Have faith. Remember Peter walking on the water? As long as he kept his eyes on the Lord, he was all right.* Trembling, Lois prayed, "I'll risk it, Lord. Just stay in sight for me."

Two months later in a quiet service in the chapel they were remarried. Several months later I met them. Lois was radiant, Roger smiling. "How is it?" I asked. "We're growing!" came the happy reply.

Lois and Roger's story contains so many beautiful elements in it that we wish it could be typical of marriages in deep trouble. Instead many end in divorce.

Perhaps one reason marriages in trouble more quickly end in divorce these days is because it is easier now to get divorces. Many Americans avoid pain, and rather than endure the pain which comes with working out differences, they think divorce is the easy way out. What they do not realize is that if they do not have the courage and faith to face the realities of the first unhappy situation, chances are they will repeat the same mistakes in the second relationship.

The fact that much of the stigma formerly attached to divorce has also disappeared contributes to more frequent divorces also. And without question TV and the movies have made their impact too. Frequent viewing of people with low moral standards, who think nothing of exchanging partners or having affairs, especially when things get tough or unpleasant at home, is sure to condition the thinking of the viewer, until at last he embraces the way of life he sees portrayed.

However, many Americans, especially those who are church

56

members, still adhere to the philosophy expressed by the African proverb: "Two civet cats, when they fight, are not to be separated." Or perhaps you have heard the answer given by a couple celebrating their 50th wedding anniversary. A reporter asked if they had ever fought.

"Of course."

"Did you ever consider divorce?"

The wife was astonished. "Divorce?" she asked. "Never!" Then, with a twinkle in her eye she added, "Murder, yes, but divorce? Never!"

Ten Ways to Strengthen Your Marriage

What can we do to enhance already happy marriages and strengthen faltering ones? Here are ten ways that have been meaningful to my husband and me.

1. *Be reasonable and realistic in your expectations of life, marriage, and your mate.*

Before I went to India as a missionary a wise man alerted me: "Your missionary career will fall into three stages. The first is the honeymoon phase when you are completely enamored with the country and the people. The second phase begins when you start to perceive shortcomings and failures in the people to whom God has called you. To your dismay you may discover they lie, cheat, steal, talk behind your back, live immoral lives, and think nothing of it. Your disillusionment may be so great you may actually find yourself hating the people, though you would never dare say so. This is a crucial stage. You may give up and go home. You may become cynical. Or you may accept them as they are and begin to love with common sense."

Most marriages go through similar stages. New love is starry-eyed and unlimited in its expectations. Many believe finding and marrying the right person will answer all of life's problems and bring the ultimate in happiness. But by mid-life we have lived through enough Saturdays and Mondays to know married life and heaven are not synonymous. We know by now that life is largely made up of routine tasks, of getting up and going to work, of paying bills and wiping up spilled milk and cleaning the house and mowing the lawn. And it is in this sphere of life we find our joyful way. We are realistic about life and reasonable in our expectations—not cynical or bitter—but reasonable.

We are reasonable and realistic in our expectations of others too. "What do you expect us to be—*perfect?*" one of our children sometimes asks me. Unfortunately all too often we demand a great deal—perhaps too much from those we love. We need to be reasonable. We do our loved ones the greatest wrong when we expect them to satisfy the deepest needs and longings of our heart. Only God can do this.

Remember in Lois and Roger's story that the relationship began to heal when Lois herself found healing in a new relationship to Christ. Christ met her deepest needs. She leaned on him. Herein lies the greatest and most lasting hope for all married couples in trouble. Efforts to bring about healing in a festering or broken relationship would do well zeroing in first on the individual's personal relationship to God. Wholeness there must come first. As we see ourselves and our failings in God's light, we become more tolerant and sensible about our expectations of others.

2. *Accept your mate as a person rather than assigning stereotyped characteristics and roles to him.*

One thing that has meant much to me in our marriage has been my husband's granting me freedom to be a person. Of course I want my husband to see me and know me first of all as a woman, but I am grateful that he also treats me as a person. He encourages me to be me, the distinct, unique human being God meant me to be. He has never forced me into either a stereotyped mold or one of his own choosing. He has respected me, valued the abilities God has given me, and encouraged me in every way to become a whole person.

I grew up at a time—at least so it seemed to me—when boys and men, as breadwinners, were considered the most important. It seemed to me too that men were expected to be always strong, disciplined, tough, aggressive, even bossy. They most surely were not supposed to cry.

58

Girls, on the other hand, "only got married." And as they became women, they were supposed to be quiet, hard-working, submissive, given to taking orders, retiring, not too ambitious.

Somewhere along the line I began to understand, however, that no one of us is 100% male (as we conceive of male) or 100% female. When I reread the verse, "In Christ there is neither male nor female," I really began to think. If I as a whole individual possess both female *and* male characteristics, then I shall experience my wholeness only as I allow myself freedom to live out both sets of characteristics—those traditionally thought of as "masculine" or as "feminine." I began to study people.

Here was John, we'll call him, a gentle, kind, sensitive man who had great gifts of love, encouragement and support. Tense, fearful people relaxed in his presence and found it easy to share their problems with him. Young people in trouble turned to him. At home John relied on mutual love to act as a deterrent to wrong action. Sometimes his children took advantage of this.

Now God, in his wisdom, had put at the side of this man a woman who was aggressive, strong, and a disciplinarian. To her fell the responsibility much of the time of "lowering the boom" on the children. To begin with she hesitated to do this, believing that in so doing she would be usurping her husband's authority. So she suppressed her impulses, tried to keep still, and in many cases, as the children took advantage of the situation, seethed inwardly with anger. Sometimes the resentment would spill over, and she would attack her husband, trying to needle him into "getting after the kids." This was entirely contrary to the man's disposition and personality. Unsure, but provoked, sometimes he would lash out at the children in an unreasoning manner, not stopping to listen first to their story. When he did this, his wife would jump in, and ask him to be just and fair. Already lacking in confidence in the role his wife was thrusting him into, he would become more unsure of himself than ever, and withdraw within himself, morose, hurt, and uncommunicative.

I watched both of them learn. The wife had to accept herself as she was. She had to stop saying, "I hate to discipline," when actually she felt far less frustrated when she could act and respond according to her temperament. She understood that to do so was not necessarily stepping into the position of head of the family; she was simply supporting and reinforcing what her husband wanted. So she was absolved of guilt feelings. She learned to accept gratefully and appreciate her husband's gentleness, patience, and kindliness—which she herself lacked. He, in turn, was grateful God had brought them together and constantly encouraged her to become the finest, most complete person she could. Respect for each other grew, and their marriage became happier. Their differences now unite them instead of dividing them.

I heard of another wife who, when she comes home from work, busies herself doing the yard work and repairing leaky faucets, while her husband dons an apron and makes dinner. Each is doing what he really enjoys doing, and both have the courage to do what they want in spite of "tsk-tsks" from others. Their permissive attitude toward each other is as refreshing as air washed free of smog after a spring rain.

Without question, a marriage is the happiest when each mate recognizes, accepts, and allows the other to be a unique individual—more than that, *encourages* the other to become the finest person he can.

3. *Husbands and wives need to be good forgivers.*

We need to for our own sakes. Even if forgiving doesn't change the one we feel has offended us, still it does change *us*.

I have a friend whose marriage has given much occasion for forgiveness on both sides. Communication still is not the best, but the situation is becoming more tolerable. And my friend is slowly discovering an inner core of peace because she is forgiving. She is not happy yet, but she is learning on some days to thank and praise God for all. And I have faith to believe that in the end the forgiving, accepting spirit she is struggling to make her habitual response will win out, and their family will know a degree of happiness they have not known before.

In her case much of the trouble stems from not having learned early in life to resolve conflicts when she encountered them. The admonition in the Bible to "not let the sun go down on your anger" is wise counsel indeed. Forgiving is best done on a daily basis. Clear the air before you go to bed and surely before you go to sleep. Don't let unconfessed and unforgiven resentments pile up. If you do, you'll soon have a high brick wall to tear down.

4. *To be happily married requires both time and effort.*

A good experience in a Christian group can be a soaring experience. Sometimes a person asks, "Why can't I achieve this warm, close, melting relationship with my mate?" Perhaps one explanation is that when we join a small group we commit ourselves to giving a sizeable chunk of time to the group. Perhaps if we gave equally as much time to our mates we would grow in a warm or more intimate relationship with each other.

I asked many middle-aged couples what they considered the single greatest factor in the breakdown of a happy married relationship. The answer given most often was "breakdown of communication."

What is to blame for lack and breakdown of communication?

"Taking each other for granted, going separate ways, and not bothering to share thoughts and feelings with each other," one said.

"The TV," many insisted.

"It's the dishwasher," one grandmother declared, wagging her finger. "Before we got the dishwasher everybody in the family had to take turns washing, wiping, and putting away. We sometimes complained, but we sure got a lot of visiting done too."

"It's snack food," another mother complained. "We sit down together for a meal only three times a week at the most."

"It's outside activities," another declared. "The Elks. The Lions. Church activities. My husband and I write notes to each other."

"Many times it's not intentional," another said. "But going to night school, working at second jobs, or husband and wife both working can contribute to it too."

A man retorted: "If women and kids were content with less, we men wouldn't have to work so hard and our women wouldn't have to work either!"

"I think a question all of us need to ask ourselves periodically in regard to our activities," one of the women said, "is, 'Is what I am doing now good for our marriage?'"

Whatever is hindering, the fact remains that good marriages, like all other excellent things, take time. What can we do about it?

One happy couple I know, Fred and Delores Allen of Garden Grove, California take a weekend away from the family every month or two. They have done this for years. "How can you afford it?" I asked. "We couldn't afford not to," they say.

Another wife greets her husband with a cup of tea when he returns from work every afternoon. The two of them spend 15 or 20 minutes together, talking, sharing. The children have grown up knowing this is Mom and Dad's time together.

Sharing work can draw a husband and wife together: work in the yard and house or sharing bookkeeping chores, letter writing, or visiting. Or perhaps they can develop new and broader avenues of service together or find something of common interest. My husband and I enjoy teaming up in Bible teaching at seminars or retreats.

Little customs, common perhaps in the early years of marriage but since forgotten, can be revived: a telephone call in the middle of the day, unexpected flowers or gifts, dressing for dinner, a ticket to a play, yes, even a new perfume.

5. *As you talk, make a conscious effort to understand one another.*

To understand and be understood is one of man's basic needs. "No one can develop freely in this world and find a full life," Paul Tournier, noted Christian doctor from Geneva, states, "without feeling understood by at least one person. Misunderstood, man loses self-confidence, he loses his faith in life or even in God. He is blocked and he regresses."

To understand what your mate is really like will require a life time. This is true because we are constantly changing. Some scholars believe our personalities change most between the ages of 25 to 35. If we cease to share with one another what we believe and how we feel about things, we will not know how the other has changed. One of the characters in Lillian Hellman's play, *Toys in the Attic*, says sadly, "Well, people change and forget to tell each other. Too bad—causes so many mistakes."

Understanding requires a lifetime also because we grow in trusting each other more. Sometimes it takes a long, long time before we dare reveal ourselves even to those we love the most.

I recall an attractive, well-educated wife of twenty years telling of an experience. She and her husband considered themselves happily married. They frequently spent hours talking and sharing. Then one day a lecturer came to their church, a quiet, perceptive man. The couple, who had known him casually before, invited him home for coffee.

"As the evening progressed and the talk deepened, I sat and listened with awe," the wife said, "as I heard my husband share dreams and hopes cherished and of encounters he had had with God about which I had never dreamed. It was as though I was listening to a stranger, and with not a little grief I wondered why he had not been able to share this with me before."

To understand another person requires first *wanting* to understand. Actually this is far more difficult than one realizes, especially if years of unhappiness, tension, and a breakdown of communication have preceded. We are all interested primarily in ourselves. To become truly interested in others requires effort. Besides, as we begin to understand another, we might see the need of *our* changing. This we do not always welcome.

But let us say we really want to understand and know the other person. What should be our next step? First, begin to pray for the person. Pray for understanding. Ask God why the other one acts and reacts like he does. Then be quiet and listen. As you do, you will be amazed how God enables you to see things from the other's perspective.

Now you are ready for step number two. Begin to listen to your mate. Listening means you first must genuinely like the person, otherwise you won't have anything to listen to! The person must know you accept and like him. Only then will he talk. If you don't really like the person, confess this to God. Ask him to change you. He can and will. He really will.

Listening means holding your tongue and not quickly responding with glib pieces of advice.

Listening sometimes means restating in your words what the other has just said. You will have to listen to be able to do this, and your friend will be reassured you are listening.

Listening means withholding judgment and criticism. Several weeks may pass before you hear the story that will explain what you have heard today. Be patient.

Listening can be done with the confident faith that you are helping the other by listening.

Listening sometimes means getting a message when no words are spoken. We need to be sensitive to moods, to expressions on faces. We learn to interpret them and become aware of needs.

As we listen, we also must begin to share. We must go beyond talking on the periphery and share the "really, really me," not fake it. It is because we haven't done this we sometimes have become very lonely.

But sharing involves risk. What if the other one does not understand? It is a risk we must take if we are to grow in understanding of each other.

One of the best ways for husband and wife to begin is by praying together. Astonishingly few couples do pray together. They may pray with their families or in other groups, but few pray together alone, just the two of them. I wonder why? Do we fear the exposure and honesty true prayer requires? Yet if we will but die to our pride in this respect, we will find new life together and with God.

I know of one young Christian couple who handle every disagreement by promptly getting down on their knees and praying together before too many angry words are spewed out.

6. *Understand what is important to your mate. Show him you care.*

Ask yourself, What can I do to make my husband's face glow with appreciation and pride? What will cause my wife to spontaneously and joyously hug and kiss me?

My husband repeatedly has encouraged me in my writing. It was he who bought my desk, filing cabinet, and even negoti-

64

ated for a larger home so I could have my own quiet study for writing.

Often we will find that what is meaningful to others doesn't cost money, only time and expression. One of my fondest memories of childhood was my father at the end of a meal reaching over to pat mother on the knee and telling her how good the meal was. No wonder our meals became more and more delicious.

Norman Vincent Peale speaks appreciatively of the neat house his wife keeps for him. For other husbands it might be as simple a thing as perked coffee instead of instant, entertaining their friends, suits in press, telephone messages promptly relayed, *not* talking to them when they first come home, cessation of nagging, no overdrawn bank accounts, peace and quiet.

However, we need to emphasize the importance of thoughtful, wise expressions of love. A woman was critically ill in the hospital for a long time. Her husband knew she had been wanting new draperies for the living room. So for her coming-home surprise he ordered new draperies. They were, however, a completely different type, color, and design from what his wife had dreamed about. She didn't like them, but was hesitant to express her feelings. In this case, letting the wife make her own selection of draperies would have been more meaningful than the element of surprise.

7. *Have a happy sex life.*

Some behavioral scientists believe we live in a time of over-emphasis on the importance of sex in married life. While that may be true of the younger generation, subjected to the emphasis of the mass media, I doubt it is true for middle-aged church people. For many of these people, and for the women especially, sex has only rarely been a pleasure. More often it is only endured. Many reasons contribute to this.

Our age put taboos on birth control devices. Fear of becoming pregnant caused many women to tense up. Again, many did not know how to express love in a spontaneous, natural way. For many, love is an intense, secret, silent emotion—whether toward God or man—and not to be expressed openly and freely and to be playful with only rarely.

It is not easy to shake loose from these inner, restraining forces. We might not even be aware of them, except we know our response is not what it could be. But even in mid-age we need a satisfying sex life. Perhaps we need it then even more than in earlier years, for the middle years can be a time of emotional impoverishment. For Mom and Dad there are no more soft little arms around the neck, no sticky kisses, no impulsive, spontaneous, "Oh, Mommie! Oh, Daddy! I love you so much!" Adolescent children, if they are still home, are reticent about demonstrating affection. Aged parents are dying. Mobility separates us from sisters and brothers and friends. "Sometimes I just ache to have someone put his or her arms around me and hold me," a middle-aged mother said to me. But men have this need too, and couples need to be aware of this need and seek to meet it for each other.

Where can we find aid so our sex life can become happier?

To grow in understanding is helpful. One book which gives much insight is *Open Marriage* by O'Neill and O'Neill, although it should be read with caution. The Christian cannot embrace the moral code the authors advocate. But surely by our middle years we should be able to read with discernment, winnowing out what is beneficial to us.

And God can liberate us as we bring the matter to him in prayer. Our heredity and environment need not determine our future for us. *God* can determine our future, if we will only let him. In mysterious ways he is able to reach into the deep recesses of our being where we are helpless to effect change and set us free. It is a work of grace. We forget his grace is available for every need. Grace, you remember, means a free, unmerited gift, given freely with no thought of return, a gift that fits our need.

Actually, as family responsibilities lessen and as the fear of unwanted pregnancies no longer lurks, sexual life in the middle years can become a more pleasurable, satisfying experience than ever before, binding very close together a man and his wife at a time in life when they need to be bound close together.

When the relationship between husband and wife becomes

better than it has ever been, the couple need not fear waning sexual desire. In fact, it is possible the desire may not wane quickly. Added pleasure will mean increased eager participation and, as in everything else, a well-oiled machine keeps running longer! And for those of us who are fighting weight gain, an added bonus, doctors tell us, is that sexual activity is a wonderful way of burning up calories. It's the one way to help keep your weight under control without denying yourself!

And as the years pass and desires do wane, the satisfied couple will not fret. They will know how to replace this with tender expressions of affection, indications of caring and thoughtful ministering to one another. These too speak the language of love.

Because unfaithfulness in marriage is ever more evident among those in the middle years, we need also to consider briefly how to handle temptation.

Temptation may come to the person in middle years because he has not understood the necessity of satisfying his continuing need for adventure. If the need for adventure is not met, frustration and boredom set in. Life becomes blah. Then it is that sometimes the need becomes so strong the person, perhaps unconsciously, seeks to satisfy the need in wrong ways. Having an affair is one of the most common.

I wonder if we do not see this illustrated in King David's affair with Bathsheba. It was the time of year for kings to go to war, we read, but David stayed home. Why? Had fighting and conquering become so common and easy to attain it no longer challenged him? Caught in boredom was he then attracted to Bathsheba?

Temptation will come also because we are capable of being attracted to many people. There is no such thing as being able to feel love and admiration for only one person. Nor is there anything sinful in attraction. Emotions are fickle. You cannot *decide* that you will not be attracted, or that you will not feel love, hate, anger, admiration, fear. These emotions will wash over you, sometimes threaten to inundate you. But you *can* control what you are going to let these emotions continue to do to you and with you.

Usually a person in the middle years cannot feel strong attraction for someone of the opposite sex without knowing it. There are a very few naive ones who do not seem to be aware of their response until they are too deeply enmeshed to get out easily. But generally speaking, a middle-aged person is neither a novice lover nor a teenager. We *know* our response. The time to nip temptation is the first moment we become aware of our response. This is difficult to do because sin is pleasurable. We want to at least play with the thought, to fantasize, to turn to it when we are bored, when our mate irritates or does not satisfy us, or before we go to sleep. Such pastime, we argue with ourselves, is innocent and harmless. Nobody will know we are doing it. We assure ourselves we have no intention of going beyond the thought.

Now this can be dangerous even for those who are happily married. For those who are not, it is like placing a pan of gasoline on a lighted stove. Not without cause did Jesus write: "Anyone who looks on a woman to lust after her in his heart has committed adultery with her already in his heart."

The temptation must be stopped with the pleasurable thought. But outward action should be taken too. Physical distance—miles —must be put between the two attracted to each other, no matter what the cost. Move the family. Change jobs. Dismiss a secretary. No sacrifice is too great. The move must be made. Separation must come about. The two should not be able to see each other. And then attention must be directed towards correcting and improving the original marriage relationship.

Maybe we have failed in not being strong enough in our insistence that temptation must be recognized and dealt with drastically *before* it becomes sin. We have become so indulgent and accepting of divorce that we let temptation walk in the door and think nothing of it till it has us trapped. Even then we are "broad-minded" and "understanding."

Admittedly, there are certain cases where divorce is the only solution. But aside from these rare cases, the marriage vows should still be regarded as binding on one for life. Divorce, in any case, is shattering. It wounds and kills. It can stunt and

68

embitter. It adds burdens to life and produces many new problems.

The Christian in his middle years who is bored or unhappy with his marriage should earnestly seek ways of bettering it rather than quickly and easily casting it aside in favor of starting afresh with another union. *If we do not have courage and faith to face our past problems and failures, chances are great we will repeat the same mistakes in a second relationship.* And today, more than ever, many stand ready to help us.

8. *Recognize that adverse situations sometimes have caused the problems that arise and stop blaming each other or yourself.*

Orin and Marlys Bennett, who have celebrated their fiftieth wedding anniversary, married when both were very young. Marlys moved in to help care for Orin's widowed father and brothers. It wasn't easy for a seventeen-year-old. "Many a night," Marlys remembers, "I cried myself to sleep on Orin's shoulder. But young though we were, we recognized the trouble wasn't between *us*. It lay in a difficult situation. After a while we were able to move into a little home of our own, and then things improved."

Sometimes a child or children can become divisive factors in a marriage. If a parent is having problems with a child, he may feel that he is out of control. This produces frustration. The frustration may be vented, not only on the child, but on the innocent mate, and the bewildered mate wonders what he did wrong now.

Learning more about each other's childhood and early years can help us understand how these too might be causing difficulties in our marriage relationship. And couples need to recognize also that great forces in our present society are at work to cause marriage relationships to disintegrate. In fact, in many cases the stresses of life have become so complex that couples will need to seek help.

9. *Find substitute extended families who can help and encourage.*

"Many hands make light work," is true in regard to the help, encouragement and support sympathetic, understanding relatives can give us in raising our families. This is true for sunny days and even more so for days of trouble.

But for many of us today hundreds, even thousands of miles, separate us from our relatives. We live as isolated family units. (The small family unit of father-mother-children is referred to as the nuclear family. The larger family which embraces grandparents, aunts, uncles and cousins, is called the extended family.) An extended family does much to strengthen the nuclear family. The children do not experience as much peer pressure from other conflicting groups when they are surrounded by cousins who are reared by the same values they are. Like-minded uncles and aunts strengthen and reinforce the parents' stand. There may be less rebellion among the children.

Often another family member will be closer in age to the child than his own parents and may understand the child better. "You don't understand me!" How often parents hear this! Sometimes parents *do* understand, but the child doesn't realize. Sometimes parents *don't* understand. Children in school often are being subjected to teachings and values so different from what their parents were that chasms of misunderstanding can develop. If small nuclear families limit themselves to their own inadequate resources, someone in the family is sure to suffer. Within the circle of a large extended family the child has far better chances of finding someone who can understand him.

Emotional needs are met. Grandparents may be more accepting, tolerant and patient than parents. They have more time to look at bugs, listen to questions, and take delight in their grandchildren. Aunts and uncles have varied interests. If they are unmarried, they often share their income with their nieces and nephews, taking them on trips and tours the parents cannot afford. During these excursions the child's life is enriched by intimate association with another family member whom he loves, trusts, and often admires.

Many of us, however, are going to have to learn to live as isolated single family units and survive. One solution is to find a substitute extended family. Our family has found it in God's people.

70

Some criticize the church saying her many activities separate and pull apart a family. Perhaps over-indulgence in church activities can contribute to this, but it has been our experience as a family that the activities and opportunities for study, worship, service, and fun which our church has offered us have strengthened our family unit.

I am grateful when my church meets some of the needs of our children which I would find difficulty meeting. I am appreciative of church school teachers who love and are tuned in to my children. I admire and appreciate youth counselors who actually enjoy overnighters with our young people, for those who accompany them to the beach for a whole day. I rejoice over the listening ears and understanding hearts our young people have found in peer friends and young adult friends at church. I am grateful to pastors who through sermons and teaching hold up the same moral standards we do and also help our children grow in faith and grace. I cheer every one who loves Jesus and encourages our children to do so. By so doing they strengthen the emphasis my husband and I have sought to give.

We also find among God's people friendship and love different from what we would experience in our home. Through sermon and Bible study our sights are being constantly lifted. We are expected to stretch and grow, so we stretch and grow. We are encouraged when down-hearted, supported in trouble, loved, and accepted. Our lives have been greatly enriched. Our marriage has become more meaningful and our family life the deeply happy and rewarding one it is largely because of our close associations with God's people which we have found usually in the fellowship of the organized church.

So while we miss our extended families and suffer some impoverishment because we are not near them, we have found a blessed substitute indeed in God's family.

10. *Set family goals.*

"Love does not consist in gazing at each other but in looking outward together in the same direction," Saint-Exupery declared.

The home and family should never become an end in itself but rather the base from where we serve God. Too much attention paid to family relationships can itself breed trouble. Why is there such a high divorce rate among marriage counselors? Could one reason be that they are always concentrating on marriage problems?

No matter how troubled or happy we are in our home relationships, we do well not to limit our interests to the home. In turning outward and in seeking to help others we, in turn, will find life. We can set family goals and then work together to accomplish those goals.

We have considered ten ways we can make a good marriage better and strengthen a weak one. Time and money we spend in solidifying our marriage will, in the end, be the greatest gift we can give our children. If we are happy together, we shall be better parents. We also shall be teaching them lessons about married life, setting patterns for them to follow.

The relationship between husband and wife is unique. Anne Morrow Lindbergh states: "It is not two exclusive people shutting out all others. It is not two turned outward though pulling together. It is rather two complete individuals facing life together."

If midway through our married years we want this to be our goal, we do well first to stop and thoughtfully and prayerfully re-evaluate our married life as it is now.

This has been a difficult chapter to write. Difficult because the subject commands the attention of a whole book, not just one chapter. But if you want to search further, I can direct you to some books which others have found helpful.

Being Married by Evelyn M. Duvall and Reuben Hill
The Creative Years by Reuel L. Howe
Married Love in the Middle Years by James A. Peterson
Gift from the Sea by Anne Morrow Lindbergh
Bed and Board, Plain Talks About Marriage by Robert Capon
Good Marriages Grow by Irene Harrell
Living on the Growing Edge by Bruce Larson

The Seasons of Life: To Understand Each Other by Paul Tournier

Success in Marriage: How to Make the Most of Your Marriage by David R. Mace.

Get them and read them later. For just now, stay on board, won't you? We're going to talk next about living with grown-up children and aging parents.

6

Developing a New Relationship with Our Children

> Believe me, it's a long apprenticeship
> learning to love.
>
> —MICHEL QUOIST

"Why do you still set a time for me to be in at night? Don't you trust me?" Nineteen-year-old Beth stood facing her mother, fingering her keys, dark eyes flashing. Beth's reaction, typical of many emerging into young adulthood, voiced the need for her parents to establish a new relationship with her.

Parents sometimes procrastinate in switching roles from controlling to supportive parent for a number of reasons, some conscious, some unconscious. Some fear it is an admission that they, the parents, are getting old. Becky, in a college class I attended, told of how her father's company always gave a Christmas dinner party for the families of the executives. Becky is eight and ten years older than her brother and sister.

"The little kids were always allowed to go to the dinner," Becky said, "but I had to stay home. This year I insisted I go. Dad's colleagues expressed surprise when they met me. Their wives said to mother, 'We didn't know you had a daughter this age!' Mother was furious with me, because she had to face up to her age."

Some parents fear losing attention, affection and assistance of their children.

"What can I do with my mother-in-law?" one young bride asked. "She calls every day. Her husband is often out of town on business, and she expects Dick, who is my husband and her son, to come over and repair every leaky faucet or clogged drain or just come and talk to her—or rather, listen to her talk. I've been thinking we should move just far enough away so a telephone call would be a toll call."

Unconsciously, perhaps, this mother felt she should be rewarded by her son for her efforts when he was a child. When he was little, she had allowed him to absorb most of her time and money. Now she feared losing his attention and affection.

Not so Mrs. Cruse Blackburn of Southern California. Blind since she was three years old, she had been dependent on her son, Raymond, since her husband died in 1971. But when Raymond wanted to marry, Cruse gladly released him. "God will have some way of looking after me," she said cheerfully.

Some parents fear that the children, lacking good judgment, will make mistakes. Strange, isn't it, how we forget that one of the ways we learn is by making mistakes. Consider the attitude of the father in the story of the prodigal son in Luke 15. Surely his wise father-mind told him his son's request was foolish. But the father knew his son would have to learn some lessons on his own, and so he not only let his son go, but gave him his inheritance.

We forget also that God has given to each of us the "right" to make mistakes. A father who had suffered heartache from the waywardness of two of his children wrote: "Parents need to learn that there comes a time in the life of every person when he has a 'right to be wrong.' Development into maturity and independence involves decision making, and always carries with it the potential of error, whether deliberate or not. Thus to be human is to have the right to be wrong. This 'right' does not make a wrong decision right; neither does it absolve from the consequences of wrong choices. But our children have the 'right to be right' and the 'right to be wrong.'"

Sometimes the child is the one reluctant to break away from his parents. Then the parents must gently push him from the nest. Sharon was only nineteen when she wanted to get married. Her parents warned her there would be problems because her fiancé, Steve, came from an entirely different background. Sharon didn't think so. Three months after their marriage Sharon showed up at home with tales of complaint against Steve.

"We think Steve is a fine young man, and evidently you do too, or you wouldn't have married him," her parents said and sent her back to Steve. And thus they nudged her from the nest when she wanted to crawl back in.

What then can we do to help our young people achieve liberation from complete dependence on us and develop into responsible adults?

1. *Constantly encourage them to become independent.*

Parents vary in the way in which they grant freedom to their children. Some are lenient when the children are young and then restrict and prohibit more and more as they get older. Others maintain the same rules throughout childhood, adolescence, and even on into adulthood. Still others apply the most restraints when the child is young and then little by little allow more and more freedom.

When the first method is followed, when a child is clamped down on more and more as he gets older and older, he is apt to erupt like a volcano. On the other hand, if the parents do not release their hold gradually, the child will feel insecure when he is pushed from the nest. "My parents did everything for me until I graduated from high school. Then suddenly they told me I was on my own," one girl confided. "I was petrified. For weeks I couldn't sleep."

"I know," another one said, "only it happened to me when I was 20. 'You're an adult now,' my parents said. Did they expect me suddenly to change overnight? If they had let me make decisions little by little and had reassured me of their help if I needed it, I would have felt much more secure."

Encouraging our eaglets to fly is a process usually requiring two decades or more in time and much love, sacrifice, patience, and understanding. When freedom is granted according to the responsibility shown, the child grows and develops into an independent young person.

Actually the parent knows we never really are independent,

but rather interdependent. He knows his child will realize this too as he matures. But the road to learning the necessity and value of interdependence is often over the bumpy, uncomfortable road of independence. Consequently, to rear a child so he becomes self-reliant and independent of his parents is one of the primary and most important tasks of a parent.

2. *Be patient and accepting even when you can't understand or agree with their behavior.*

They might not be as demonstrative of their love and affection as they were formerly. "Don't kiss me!" we'll hear, maybe even, "Don't touch me!" Their remarks might make us feel as though we have leprosy; but we shall have to remind ourselves that when our children utter these stay-away warnings, it isn't because they love us the less, but because they are trying to break their dependence on us. It may hurt when we see them pouring out their affection on their friends and possibly even on some older friends whom they have chosen to be their confidantes. The temptation will come to feel slighted, unloved, unappreciated, but we need to withstand the temptation to tears, complaining, or self-pity of any kind. Nor should we insist they show us affection, but instead rejoice that our children truly are maturing.

Our growing children might not confide in us as much any more. "Don't ask me!" "Forget it!" "You wouldn't understand!" "Leave me alone, won't you?" Over and over we may hear this. We need to respect this desire on their part for privacy and their desire to work things out on their own.

One mother noticed how her adolescent daughter would begin to share and then abruptly stop. Finally she asked her daughter why she stopped. "Oh," said the girl shrugging, "it sounds silly when I say it. You wouldn't understand."

In her teens this sensitive woman had been bereaved of her mother. With no one to confide in she had poured out her woes into her diary. She had kept the diary. She dug it out now. "Maybe this would interest you," she said casually to her daughter. After that mother became a more frequent confidante.

But if the young adult chooses not to confide, father and

mother do well not to question, probe, or demand they be told everything.

Young adults might exaggerate. Before you get furious about something they have said, go into your room and rock for a while in your rocking chair. Ask yourself if they have exaggerated for effect's sake. A friend of mine told of overhearing a telephone conversation of her daughter.

"Oh, your mom got all upset, did she?" Silence. "That's too bad." Silence. "My mom? Naw, she knows I mean only a fourth of what I say."

Well, thought that mother, *I hadn't known that before, but I'm sure glad to learn it now.*

Their grooming habits might irritate us. When young people choose to dress and groom themselves in a different fashion, parents protest, explode, ridicule, demand reformation, suffer in martyr-like silence, ignore not only the style of dress but also the young person himself, resign themselves to it, or strike a compromise—some even adopt the fashions themselves. Perhaps the happiest route lies in recognizing that both parents and children have "rights."

After a year away from home Tom moved back to attend a community college. "His casual dress was hard for us to accept," his mother confessed. His long, unkempt hair particularly annoyed my husband. Finally my husband said, 'Look, son, I can stand to sit and look across the table at long hair, but I can't stand it when it's uncombed. Either comb it or eat your meals on a tray in your room.' Tom sputtered and then began to comb his hair."

Our children might not adopt our values. "What do you do," a tall, graying, highly intelligent man asked, "if your children scorn and ridicule what you hold dear?" He was touching on what can be a very sore point especially for fathers.

The wrong reaction, of course, is to despair. True, when a father cannot look at his children and see in them that which satisfies him, and when he feels completely helpless and frustrated in doing anything about this, he is tempted to despair. He may mask his despair with disgust—or a thousand little disgusts, expressed towards the child. The child, it seems, can do nothing to please him. Or the father may revert to sulking and acting like a selfish child himself. Or he may identify with his child, against his own convictions, adopting his child's standards and philosophy as his own, when in reality they are not. But when a middle-aged person reverts to adolescent behavior or thought, it works havoc with his integrity.

But what can a parent do?

In the first place, we need to re-examine what we claim to be our set of values and the actual way in which we live our lives. We cannot hold double standards. As our children observe day by day how we live and talk and act, they will pick up the values we model. We cannot say to our child, "Don't drink. Don't smoke," if we drink and smoke. If we want them to show appreciation and gratitude, we need to ask ourselves, "Do they see me expressing appreciation?" If we want them to be free of the lust for money and material things, we shall have to examine ourselves as to how much desire for these actually do control *our* life. *Why* are we working? So, in some cases, if we see our children adopting values with which we are not happy, we may have to say, "I'm going to stop some of the crazy things I've been doing." And in some cases if they adopt values different from ours we may have to be humble enough to ask, "Who is choosing more wisely, they or we?"

3. *Maintain an attitude of love and trust rather than of guilt and worry.*

Many parents suffer guilt because they wonder if they raised their children in the right way.

"We had five children," one woman said, "and they were just far enough apart in years so all five have been brought up in a different way, depending on which method of child rearing was in vogue when the child was born. Goodness knows which method was best or if any of them was any good."

There's little point in fretting about the past. If you did your best, leave it in God's hands. He has a way of compensating for our mistakes.

But what do you do when you *know* you've made mistakes in

raising your children? "I came to know Christ only a couple of years ago," one mother said. "If I had known him earlier, I would have taught my children altogether different values."

The answer is: live Christ now. Your children will see the difference he has made in you.

"I've been a Christian all our married life," another mother said, "but that doesn't mean I've done everything right. I sometimes became very irritated and even angry with my children. Sometimes I punished them unjustly. When I think of it, I feel so guilty."

How good it is to know that not only does God forgive us, but he also enables our children to recover from injury and to make adjustments. As Reuel Howe expresses in his book *The Creative Years:* "The mistakes we make are not nearly as powerful as the love we give." Friends of ours have seen this truth beautifully portrayed.

They adopted a two-year-old boy who had been mistreated severely as a baby. Wounded and hurt, he would lash out at them. Feeling insecure, he would do anything he could to get attention, and one of the most effective ways was by being mean. Though they tried to offer him affection, he did not know how to accept or return love. Sometimes his hostile and contentious behavior caused his mother's patience to run thin. Then she would speak too harshly, downgrade him—though she knew this was the exact opposite of what he needed—or punish him in anger. Minutes later, in remorse, she would weep. But always she loved the child passionately and yearned for him. When she wronged him, she went to him and asked his forgiveness and always received it. On his 19th birthday the son wrote: "God has given me the very best parents I could have ever asked for. I want to thank you for bringing me up, and I want you to know I love you very much. Sure there have been hassles, but we expect them."

Many parents today are struggling with guilt feelings as their children give birth to babies out of wedlock or divorce after only a few years of married life. "What did we do wrong?" they cry.

Maybe nothing. We need to remember that though we can

81

influence and guide, the final choice rests with the child. As we said before, we have to give our children the same right God gives us, the right to choose.

But if we are not to feel guilty, what should be our response to a child who has deeply hurt us? The father of two wayward children referred to earlier says: "The Christian parent will continue to hold on to his child, come what may, with the bonds of faithful love. Parents can perhaps, if they wish, permit the hard experience of life to 'kill' their love for a child who has spitefully used them. But, conversely, they can, if they will, continue to love that wayward individual in the hope (maybe it will prove vain) that he will some day respond and that some day reconciliation will occur.

"A parent with a Christian perspective knows something about the unselfishness of the love of God for his wayward children. Such was the love which prompted him to send to earth his Redeemer-Son and which moves his Spirit to work continuingly in his erring children for their forgiveness and spiritual growth. This is the kind of love which Christians are exhorted to reveal in their dealings with other people, pure, unselfish love, never achieved by humans but always worth the effort. The forgiven— unto seventy times seven—are in turn forgivers—unto seventy times seven."

"Joan came home five months pregnant," one mother said. "She wanted to keep her baby, but neither the boy who was the baby's father or she wanted to marry. What were we to do? The baby was born, a beautiful, healthy child. Now Joan wants to go back to college and make something of her life. I'm caring for the baby. Of course, I wish circumstances had been different, but I'm rather enjoying having a baby to care for again. And Joan loves her baby dearly, because she feels God used the whole circumstance to help her get right with him and get her values straightened out."

"I was heartbroken when Annie told me she was pregnant," another mother, herself a widow, confessed. "But how could I turn Annie out on the street? A short while later I came down with an illness that kept me in bed for months and months. How grateful I was for Annie's loving care of me. The baby was born. I recovered and went back to work. What a treat it was to come home every evening to a sparkling house, a hot dinner, laundry done and a cooing grandson! Now that he is older we have him in a Christian nursery, and Annie is back at college. We're believing roses will bloom out of the ashes."

When a divorced daughter or son comes home with small children and all the attendant problems, parents find themselves really cast on God to understand what is the Christian way to respond. They forgive, love, and accept, yes—but does their responsibility end with this, or are they expected to raise another family just when they were looking forward to years of more freedom? How good that God has promised us wisdom, each of us in our individual, differing situations.

Another heartbreaking situation arises when children leave or run away from home and never contact their parents. Then to hang on in love and trust is an acid test. The parents will be tempted to think the child cherishes no love or gratitude towards them at all. At times like this we need to cling to the fact that it is almost impossible to kill a child's love for his parents.

"It's an odd psychological fact," a counselor at a home for juvenile delinquent boys told me, "but boys who have nothing to go back to at all get really homesick and want to return home."

Now if this is true for children who have been mistreated, how much stronger must be the love ties where the home atmosphere has been warm and accepting. So form a mental image of the kind of person you want your son or daughter to become (hopefully, you will let God direct your desires). Focus on that image. Thank God it will be so. And then begin to treat your young person as the responsible individual you believe he will become.

4. *Above all, don't let relationships rupture.*

Emily, a mother of several young adult children, tells her story:

"Virginia was dating a divorced man considerably older than she. He had custody of the two children from his previous marriage. Other factors caused us concern also. Their racial and cultural backgrounds were very different. We talked and talked with Virginia. It got us no place. So we prayed God would stop the marriage. But though I prayed and prayed, I could get no assurance God would answer my prayer. My frustration mounted. The relationship with our daughter worsened to the point where Virginia moved out. I continued to pray. Finally it occurred to me I should change my prayer. I began to pray that the good relationship we had had with Virginia before would be restored. Immediately I was assured I was praying for the right thing. My attitude changed, and Virginia's did also. We were reconciled. In the end she did marry, and the marriage is a happy one. Her husband has become a dedicated Christian, and our relationships have never been better."

Walls often come between parents and children when the young people go away to college, especially if neither parents or children write or call.

"Our son never writes," a troubled mother told me. "He used to call collect. Last time when he did, his father asked him why he didn't write. Joe said there wasn't anything that would interest us. That really made my husband blow up. He told me not to accept any more pay calls from him."

"And you?"

Her eyes dropped to the floor. "I stopped writing too."

"But you're unhappy about it?"

"Of course. He's coming home in a couple weeks' time for Christmas, and his father is ready to blister him."

Here is a situation where the parents can determine the future of their relationship with their child. Being a parent calls for infinite patience. Sometimes we need to go not only the second mile, but the third and fourth too. A guiding question to ask ourselves is: what can I do in order that the relationship between our child and us be the best it can possibly be? If we keep in view our ultimate goal, a continuing good relationship with our child, it will help us see present difficulties in perspective, and we shall discover we can afford to be generous and forgiving. Time matures all of us. With maturity comes a different point of view. Sometimes it takes longer for some to mature than others. Then we have to wait. And show our maturity.

The father of an able, young doctor tells of how when his son

84

left for college, he tossed him a couple of quarters. "If you need me, call," he said. Years later, the night of the boy's wedding, as the son was saying goodbye to his father, he tossed his dad two quarters. The father fingered them, then with a smile tossed them back. A few weeks later the son bumped into a problem and called his father. "That would never have happened," the father said, "if the quarters hadn't kept the way open all the previous years.

It will be worth every effort to maintain good relationships with our children. In the years ahead we shall need them, and they will need us.

5. *Be thankful for the help others give.*

We are not alone. Good teachers play an important role. A trusted pastor can become a true friend. Or our young adult children may seek out other older adults to whom they feel free to confide. Don't be jealous of these relationships. Welcome them. Encourage them. Others can make our job easier.

6. *Remember that in the end our children are God's.*

Have we given them to him? Then we can trust him and never give up hope.

7. *Appreciate them.*

Appreciate them for the joy, freshness, and vigor they bring to a home. Appreciate them for the help their strong, young arms and untiring bodies can give. Appreciate them for their skills and abilities manifested in song and music, in art and crafts, in baking, cooking and sewing, in carpentry and painting. Appreciate them for their keen discernment, their glowing idealism. Appreciate them for their warm love for Jesus, for kindnesses they show others, for compassion. Appreciate them for their knowledgeable conversation, spiked with humor and colorful language, seasoned with a reflective thought you wouldn't have guessed them capable of yet. Appreciate them for the loyal, clear-eyed friendship they offer you. Appreciate them when they correct you or point out your inconsistencies. Appreciate them for being themselves, unique, marvelous individuals. Appreciate them, and in your bedroom at night, as you and your mate share the joy they have brought you that day, smile in the dark and say, "How could we ever have brought such lovely persons into being?"

As your heart is warmed, you will discover a wonderful miracle taking place. *You* are being appreciated.

My husband, Luverne, while speaking at a conference, was staying in the home of one of the pastors. One morning Luverne came into the living room to find the pastor vigorously blowing his nose. "Read this," he said, handing a letter to my husband. "It's from Carol. She's at college."

The letter read in part:

Dear Ones,

I may not have been the best correspondent this year, but I want you all to know that each year I am away, you become dearer to me. I love you for what you are and what you have helped me become. For our wonderful closeness of family ties, I am very grateful . . . For all your warmth and sincerity, for the love you have given so freely, for the happy and trying times we've shared, for everything you are and represent to me in high ideals and fine living, for the joy of being part of such a wonderful family—I thank our Father above! Not only now, but always, you are in my heart, because you are part of me!

With tenderness,

Carol

As we genuinely appreciate our young people and express our appreciation, a bonus for them will be the flowering of self-confidence. They will need self-confidence. They will need to be assured they are of value, that they can find their place in society and become contributing members, that they can control the controllable factors in life. They will need this if they are going to take wings and fly, to swoop and soar and rise above the problems and pettiness of our troubled old world.

As helpers and guides, acknowledging our common humanity and weaknesses, mutually turning to God from whom all love and faith comes, we as parents in our middle years can work thus for new relationships that will encourage our eaglets to fly.

If your children are teenagers still you may enjoy Dr. Haim G. Ginott's book *Between Parent and Teenager*. Getting together and talking with other parents of teenage children can be immensely helpful also. You'll discover neither you nor your kids are as strange or abnormal as you had begun to think.

Getting Along with Your Grown-up Children by Helene Arnstein is also a helpful book.

To Think About

1. How would I rate my relationship with each of our children now?

very good	good	acceptable
could be better	strained	broken

2. What can I do specifically to improve relationships with each one?

7

Caring for Aging Parents

> *Kindness should begin at home, support-*
> *ing needy parents. This is something that*
> *pleases God very much.*
>
> —1 TIMOTHY 5:4 (LIVING BIBLE)

Phyllis handed a gaily checked apron to her mother.

"Busy day ahead," she said briskly. "Wash and dry the dishes. Put them away. Guests are coming tonight. We'll go to the market. Later you can make a cole slaw for dinner."

Phyllis' mother responded with a smile and hummed as she washed the dishes. Phyllis brought an armful of laundry from her mother's room and loaded the washer. She tapped her mother on the shoulder and smiled. "Time for the first walk of the day," she said, motioning toward the bathroom. With guests coming tonight I'll have to be especially mindful today and remind her, Phyllis thought, and I'll have to check for unintentional messes.

Dishes done, the two drove to a shopping center. After the marketing Phyllis remembered she had a check to cash. "Wait in the car," she said to her mother. "I'll be right back."

The lines in the bank were longer than Phyllis had expected. As she stood waiting a woman came up to her. "Was it your mother waiting for you in the car? She's wandering around, looking for you."

"Oh, no!" Phyllis exclaimed and dashed out to find her wandering aimlessly about on the parking lot. *I won't be able to leave her any more*, Phyllis thought, on the way home.

At home Phyllis shampooed and set her mother's hair. Then she phoned for the sitter for her mother they would need Thursday night when they went out. After her mother's nap Phyllis helped her mother bathe and laid out the clothes her mother would be wearing for dinner.

That evening after the guests had gone, in the refuge of their bedroom Phyllis collapsed on her husband's shoulder. "It isn't that I don't love mother and want to care for her," her words were muffled. "It's just that it's not always easy. If she's going to keep in touch with reality, she needs to be with people. But tonight especially it was hard including her in the conversation. After I had had her tell Mrs. Brooks how she makes her cole slaw—and mother's cole slaw is delicious—I was at a loss to know what other subjects to introduce." She blew her nose and straightened. "And then when you came home the last minute and told me two extra guests were coming, and I had pie only for six I wanted to tell you right then and there how upsetting this is for me. But I didn't dare. Not in front of mother. She might misunderstand and think *she* had done something to upset me."

"You can tell me off now," her husband said grinning.

"That's the trouble," Phyllis was laughing and crying. "I don't feel like doing it now!"

Phyllis' situation is typical of many middle-aged "children" who have loved and cared about their parents and who now, at a time in life when they had looked forward to a little freedom, find themselves having to care *for* their parents. What does it involve? What needs do aging parents have?

A home to live in. Work to do. Children who love and care. These are basic.

A Home to Live In

Generally, old folks stay younger and are happier in their own homes. If they need help, there are ways you can help:

- hiring someone to do weekly cleaning or laundry or yard work
- bringing over hot meals or arranging for meals on wheels

- helping with repairs, window washing, putting up storm windows, etc.
- installing a telephone by their bed, then having someone call them regularly
- helping with grocery shopping and transportation
- if needed, arranging for a home health aide to call regularly
- visiting regularly or writing
- if their budget is limited, augment it by supplying things they use and need regularly
- showing affection.

A friend of mine, Hazel, found many ways to lovingly care for her invalid mother when she chose to stay on in their own home. Fortunately, Hazel's father was exceptionally skilled in giving his wife nursing care, so this was a great help. But Hazel went every day (except when they were out of town) for six years to visit her mother. She did her laundry, ran errands, shopped, shampooed and set her mother's hair at home or took her to a beauty shop, baked and cooked for her.

"But I was happy to do it," my friend insists. "Caring for mother was a rewarding experience. To begin with I wondered where I would find time to do all the extras. I have an active family and handle the office work of my husband's business. But God always gave me strength, patience, and the listening capacity I needed."

If your parents want to move to another part of the country, suggest they rent first. They should make sure they like the new setting before they settle there permanently.

If aging parents want to move out of their own home and live somewhere else other than with you, there are many alternatives to choose from:

- motor homes in which to travel
- mobile homes, stationary in courts
- apartment hotels (some are operated by churches)

- board and care homes
- private retirement homes
- retirement homes operated by churches
- private homes.

For information on low cost financing available through the Department of Housing and Urban Development, write to them at Washington, D.C. for their pamphlets: *Homeownership for Lower Income Families, a Rural Credit Program; Home Ownership, Mobile Home Financing Through HUD.*

The Mobile Homes Manufacturers Association (Box 56066, Chicago, Ill. 60656) publishes many booklets like "Financing and Insuring Your Mobile Home."

Woodall's *Directory of Mobile Home Communities* rates approximately 12,000 mobile home communities, gives information on financing, insurance, laws, and regulations for every state.

If your parents have come to the place where they can no longer carry on independently and you are wondering what to do, answering the following questions might shed some light as to what course you should follow. Ask yourself:

1. How much will they let me do? Will they let me make plans for them?
2. How much can they do for themselves?
3. How much can they afford?
4. How much can we afford?
5. What are we able to do for them? How is our health?
6. Would we be able to get along together if we lived together?
7. Would they like to live where we live and would they like our way of living?
8. Are the plans we are considering ones that we can follow for several years?

If parents and children find it difficult to get along when they live together, can arrangement be made for the parents to live with someone else? Sometimes this works out better.

And what shall we do if the the day comes when they need a nursing home? So many critical articles have been written on nursing homes that a negative public attitude has been created. Many people are living alone in misery, afraid that a nursing home might be even worse. Relatives of those who live in nursing homes often suffer needlessly from a sense of guilt. As one director of retirement homes confesses, "Certainly there are people in nursing homes who are miserable, but this is also true of those in hospitals. The fact is these people are less miserable and have a better chance for a brighter future because of the nursing home. In many nursing homes fantastic progress is being made, not only in the quality of nursing care but in the area of spiritual and social components of care."

Another director said: "If physical care makes life possible, psycho-social care makes life worthwhile," and added that it is this aspect that is being emphasized especially in the homes sponsored by churches. Almost every city of any size will have a church-sponsored home where you may be assured your loved one will receive loving care. Contact your pastor. He can give you guidance.

Typical of a home where the Christian atmosphere pervades every facet of life are the 146 facilities owned and operated by the Evangelical Lutheran Good Samaritan Society, Sioux Falls, S.D. One of their larger complexes (they tend to emphasize smaller, more home-like units in neighborhoods where the retired people have spent their lives) is the Good Samaritan Village in Hastings, Nebraska. This bustling retirement center houses almost 1300 residents. The village, located on 90 acres, has more than 700 apartment units, paved streets and sidewalks, all utilities and even a small lake. Seven levels provide care for the residents: one-, two- or three-bedroom apartment units, for self-sustaining couples or individuals; similar apartments for those who can maintain their own household with some assistance from a house visitor; accommodations for those who need a meal a day served to them in the common dining room or brought to them in their apartments; facilities for couples who can no longer maintain their own households; care homes for people who are up and about but need supervision and meals; and the infirmary for those in wheelchairs or walkers or in need of total bed care.

The waiting lists at church-sponsored homes often is long, so if you can anticipate your needs, get your name on the waiting list early.

In addition to church-sponsored homes, there are many excellent private nursing homes also.

If you are considering a retirement center for your parents or choosing a home, it might be helpful to consider these points:

1. Is it clean? well-ventilated? well-lighted?
2. Ask to see a week's menu.
3. Is medical care available?
4. Become acquainted with those operating the home.
5. Is it near churches, shopping, etc.?
6. Do guests have freedom?
7. Will your parent have a room alone or share?
8. Does the home provide entertainment?
9. May the residents have guests?
10. What does it cost?

If you decide to take your parents into your home, you might find it helpful to read *You and Your Aging Parents* by Edith M. Stern with Mabel Ross, M.D.

Work to Do

Facts revealed in a study by the University of Southern California School of Gerontology show there is a great need for self-esteem among senior citizens. Self-esteem can be gained through working with and for others. It brings a sense of fulfillment and enhances physical and spiritual well-being.

Aging parents who live close to married sons and daughters or their own sisters and brothers often find that reaching out a helping hand can be immensely satisfying. Many older people find joy in participating in volunteer programs. Churches, hospitals and communities have volunteer programs. The opportunities for service are unlimited.

In 1972 Mrs. Pearl Williams of Los Angeles, a mere 103, was honored as the oldest foster grandparent in the nation. She cares for two children four hours daily, five days a week at the Willows

Residence School and Day Center in Compton. Her "children" are physically and mentally handicapped. Mrs. Williams feeds and dresses them, plays games with them, and gives them individual attention. In return she receives a small weekly salary, transportation, a hot lunch, and a lot of satisfaction. The service is part of the Older Americans Volunteer Programs for men and women over 60 with an annual income below $2000 for single persons and $2600 for couples.

If parents are receptive to the idea of doing volunteer work, the middle-aged "child" can help by passing on information as to opportunities that exist, by providing or arranging for transportation if needed, by taking an interest in what the parents are doing. But final decisions, of course, are Mom and Dad's. They know best what they enjoy doing and what they want to do and surely at this time in life they shouldn't have to be subjected to being "bossed around."

Children Who Love and Care

How do you say "I love you?" to your parents?

An ancient letter tells us how. It describes an unusual love affair. The chief character in the story was a wizened, scarred old man. He couldn't even support his beloved; in fact, his beloved was supporting him. He was, you see, a jailbird.

His affair was not just with one fair lady either, but rather with some touchy, quarrelsome old ladies and some men too!

The love affair was being sustained through letters, for lover and beloved were separated by many miles. One of these love letters has survived. We know it as the epistle Paul wrote to the congregation at Philippi, and it is to this letter we turn now to learn how to say, "I love you."

1. *Say it.* To say, "Of course they know I love them" is not enough. Paul reveals his affection for the Philippians in his letter: "I hold you in my heart," he writes. And again: "I yearn for you." "My beloved." "My brethren, whom I love and long for."

When we are not limited to communicating through letters, we can say "I love you," not only with words, but also by touch and looks. Put your arms around your aging parents. Hug them. Pat them. Kiss them. Stroke their hair. Joke with them. Tease them gently and lovingly.

2. *Love, not only in word, but also in deed.*

In the case of Paul and the Philippian Christians the love between them was not simply an exchange of sentimental words either. Paul had suffered to see the Philippian Christians introduced to God.

They, in turn, tried to understand what Paul's needs were. Even Paul struggled with balancing his budget. The Christians at Philippi offered to help. Usually Paul preferred paying his own way, but he felt so close to the Philippians that he accepted their help.

At the time he wrote this letter Paul was an imprisoned man. Some Bible scholars believe respected prisoners like him were not put behind bars but rather confined to his house. For Paul, this very likely meant renting a house. The Philippian congregation sent money for rent. They also sent one of their own, Epaphroditus, to be with Paul. Money could pay the rent and buy groceries. But feet and hands were needed to bring the groceries home. And a cheerful, courageous heart was needed to encourage the aged Paul.

Our gift-giving to our aging parents should be equally thoughtful. For years my mother has pleaded with us not to buy her any more "things." "The house is full," she explains. "There's no room to put any more."

But she welcomes shrubs and flowers for the garden, an airline ticket to visit us, trips to new, unexplored, and old familiar places. Mother also loves to entertain—even at 80 plus—and one year my sister-in-law gave her a big box of gaily decorated napkins for all occasions.

3. *Express appreciation to your parents for all they have done for you and have meant to you.*

Gratefully Paul acknowledges the gifts from the Philippians. "I am thankful for your partnership." "It was kind of you to share my trouble." "The gifts you sent were a fragrant offering."

What do you appreciate most about your parents? As a young

96

person I was restless, and my wanderings took me far from home. One day 2000 miles from home, my heart welled up with love for my father and appreciation for all he had meant to me. Impulsively I sat down and wrote a letter. When he received it, mother told me later, Dad read and reread it. And then, holding it in his hand he said, "We should frame this." A few months later my father was dead. I've always been glad I wrote that letter.

4. *Try to understand what is important to your parents.*

The Philippian Christians understood that not only material things were important to Paul. He admonished the Philippians, "Stand firm in the Lord." They fulfilled Paul's desire. They stood firm. And they were successful also in keeping their children true to the Lord and passing on to them their own gracious spirit of hospitality.

What is important to your parents? That the family name continue to be held in high esteem? That family solidarity continue? Has your father been a career man in the service of his country? Have your parents worked hard to support certain philanthropic causes? Have they been devout Christians, concerned that all their children live godly lives?

As you consider their interests and concerns, is there anything you can do to perpetuate them? An aging person needs to feel, not only that he has made a contribution to society, but that his influence will continue to be felt.

5. *Build and nourish confidence and faith.*

Paul's strong confidence and faith in what God could do for the Philippians is echoed again and again in the letter. "I am sure he who began a good work in you will bring it to completion." "God is at work in you, both to will and to work." "Let those of us who are mature be thus minded; and if in anything you are otherwise minded, God will reveal that to you also." "My God will supply every need of yours."

Our aging parents need to have their faith and trust nourished and strengthened. The dying of friends and relatives and their own failing health and declining strength will remind them that death, the great final test, is drawing near. To face death

97

courageously and cheerfully calls for faith, confidence, and assurance. We can help our parents build faith. If we haven't done so previously, we can talk with them as to whether they are at peace with God and man. If they need transportation, we can make arrangements so they can get to worship services. We can read and pray with them, give them records and tapes. As we reminisce with them over all the way God has led and cared for us, we can reassure one another that God will continue to care for us, that he will not forsake us. All of us, no matter how strong we have been, need this ministry from others of encouragement and faith-building. Our parents perhaps were the first ones to teach us to trust in God. Now, in gratitude we can reach out in love and strengthen their faith and confidence in God.

As our trust in God grows, peace and joy will garrison our hearts. Read through the epistle to the Philippians and count how many times the word "joy" and "rejoice" appear. Remember these expressions of joy came from a man chained to a guard day and night, from one who never knew when the summons to death would come. But he could rejoice because he was assured of God's love. He knew of God's love through the death of God's Son on the cross, true, but he also experienced God's love through the Philippian Christians. When trials and troubles come, we may always be assured, through God's Word, of his love and support. But it sure helps when others also tell us they love and care! God loves people through people. God can love your aging parents through you. So tell them you love them. Show them you love them. Express your appreciation. Value their contributions to life. Reaffirm faith in God.

Broken Relationships Hinder the Flow of Love and Need to Be Mended

Sometimes, however, people carry over into their middle years resentments and ill feelings toward their parents which have smouldered since childhood and which hinder happy relationships. A friend of mine tells how it was for her.

"Although I had every reason to be happy what with a

98

thoughtful husband, three lovely children and a beautiful home, yet I wasn't. I cried every day. Why, I didn't know.

"One day my pastor noticed my despondency. But I wasn't ready to talk. Three weeks passed. My tears and depression became so bad that finally I went to see my pastor. We talked for three hours, and I cried the whole time.

"Pastor asked me to pray God would reveal to me what my real problem was. I was to come back in a week's time.

"As I prayed, the mistreatment I had received from my father during my childhood and my resulting hatred of him kept coming back to mind.

"When I went back, pastor asked if anything had been revealed to me. I said yes, but I couldn't tell him what. Then all of a sudden I burst into tears and sobbed out the whole story. From that moment my attitude towards my father changed. I went home happier than I could ever remember being. Compassion, forgiveness and love for my father began to flow into my heart. So great was the change that pastor could see it written all over my face when I went to see him again.

"God's spirit had to change my feelings. On my own I couldn't. Through God's grace I was able to write to my father and tell him I loved him and ask him to forgive me for all the ill feelings I had cherished against him. I began to pray that my parents would have this same relationship with God that had become mine.

"A few years later my parents came to visit us. I was able to really talk to my father for the first time. I told mother how God had helped me and how personal he had become to me, how he had cleansed me of my sin and given me a new nature and made me a new person in Christ. Before my mother left to return home she made a commitment to Christ. She is now growing as a beautiful Christian.

"A year later my father was told he had cancer. He started going to church and gave his life to Christ. I can rest easier now knowing both my parents are in God's hands. I thank God continually for opening my eyes and bringing about reconciliation between my parents and me."

When family relationships are not what they should be, one warning signal may be our own inner unhappiness and depression. Resentment and anger, even when suppressed, drain us emotionally, leaving us dry and empty. When we thus overspend our emotional energy, depression often follows. So when depression persists, we do well to ask ourselves first: what has drained me emotionally? As we trust the Holy Spirit, he will bring to mind things we may have forgotten. It might be a fractured relationship which needs to be mended.

Unfortunately, we often have to be desperate before we are ready to take action. When my friend's pastor first asked her what was troubling her, she was not ready. Three more miserable weeks had to pass before she was willing to be helped.

The first glimmer of light came when she was able to pinpoint the cause of the broken relationship. As she thought back to her childhood, she realized her basic sin had been lack of love for her father. Instinctively she realized when she asked him for forgiveness, she must be careful not to blame him, not to say, "I'm sorry I cherished such resentments toward you, *but* you really were very mean to me." Instead she said simply, "God has shown me how wrong it has been on my part not to love you. I want to ask you to forgive me."

Sensitivity. Patience. Wisdom. Love. All of these we need as we care about and care for our aging parents.

As we care for them, we can bear in mind that in this area too we are setting examples, laying patterns. Some day *we* will be the aging parents. The care we receive then may well be the kind of care we give now.

8

Single Life in the Middle Years

> To be free, to be able to stand up and
> leave everything behind—without look-
> ing back. To say Yes.
>
> —DAG HAMMARSKJOLD

Emerging as a rapidly growing minorities community in the western world are the singles: the single-singles or those who have never married; the separated, divorced or deserted, the unwed mothers and fathers, and the widows and widowers. Life for many of them is bitterly difficult. They face snarled problems: financial, legal, social and personal.

In the U.S. alone they number 49 million. Their numbers are growing faster than the general population growth. During the last decade the U.S. population, as a whole, increased by 16%. The population of the unmarried shot up 38% and that of the divorced and widowed 34%. Half were over 35 years of age. Widowers over 45 number two million. Single-parent families enclose 54 million. Most of the growth in this last figure has resulted from the sharply spiraling rise in divorces.

Whether divorced, widowed, or never married, many singles find themselves wrestling with problems for which they had little or no preparation.

Problems of the Divorced or Widowed

Emotional Problems. The emotional upheaval of the divorced and bereaved rips them open. One woman, describing her divorce said: "I felt so fragile, like an open, walking sore."

Another, three years after her divorce, simply shook her head and said, "It's still too painful to talk about."

"I knew there would be problems," admitted a mother of three, whose former husband was an alcoholic, "but I never dreamed they would be as critical or overwhelming. At times I've been tempted to despair."

Financial Problems. Almost all families who lose a parent find their expenses climb and their income drops.

"Financially, it's disaster!" one mother of three, living in an older tract suburban house, declared. The sweep of her arm indicated the worn furnishings. "I don't know when we'll ever be able to replace this furniture. We should move into a newer home. This house and neighborhood are rapidly deteriorating. The money I have in the house is losing its value every year. But I can't afford buying and selling costs, bigger monthly payments, and a higher interest rate. I'm thankful I can meet my present payments. My six-year-old car sputters and misses. When it finally stops, I don't know what I'll do . . ."

"When my husband walked out on me, he left me hundreds of dollars on our credit cards to pay for," another divorcee said. "I sold our house and moved into a small apartment."

"It's been medical bills for me," a widow said. "My husband's lingering illness totalled over $10,000."

Usually widows receive help from the husband's insurance policies, pensions, Social Security benefits, and family savings. In some cases such ample provision has been made that the family is comfortably cared for. But in other cases the drop in the standard of living is like the swift descent of an elevator in a 20-story building.

But even then the financial situation of widows is usually more stable and certain than the income of divorcees. Although the law states that alimony should be provided for children until they are 18, statistics show that 90% default in their payments.

"A divorcee can consider herself lucky if she gets financial help for two years," a lawyer said. "Most marriages that break up have experienced financial difficulties prior to the legal divorce.

102

Having two households to support later only complicates the situation."

The result is that most widows and divorcees with families go job hunting. The Women's Bureau of the Labor Department reports that 53% of female heads of families are in the labor market. Many have had little or no training. Others have not worked for so many years that their skills are rusty. If they are professional people, they may find themselves almost hopelessly behind the times. A middle-aged nurse, taking a concentrated course to update her on medical techniques, held in her hand a two-inch thick blue book. "These are the drugs I have to become familiar with," she said. "Ninety percent of them have been discovered in the last 10 years. And it's 20 years since I nursed."

In situations where women find their training lagging, the median income for them in 1971 came to $5114, little more than half of the $9208 income for single-parent families headed by white men. For black women it was even worse—$3645!

The single biggest expense next to house payments and food often is care for children. Costs can run as high as $1500 a year. Added to this is the difficulty of finding good day-care centers. There are slightly over half for the number of children who need them. Both the federal government and churches are providing ways to assist these working women by establishing good day care centers and by subsidizing the cost involved.

Divorcees and widows also are often considered poor risks and find it difficult to get credit cards. "I just keep on using my husband's," one widow said.

"I can cope with everyday expenses," one mother said, "but when an appliance breaks down or I see paint peeling off the house, I get a hollow, sick feeling in my middle. I just can't afford to hire someone to do my work, and I'm limited, both in my skills and in my time."

But financial worries aren't the only ones. An even more anxious one is concern for the children.

Concern for the Children. Some authorities link the rising divorce rate with the doubling of juvenile court cases from 1960 to 1971.

"Maybe," a judge said, "but I wonder if we don't have almost as many cases from homes where husband and wife continue to live together but fight all the time. And thousands of youngsters survive divorce or death of a parent very well."

But even though the children do not get involved in juvenile court, other troublesome problems often rear their heads: anxiety, guilt, insecurity, resentment, hostility, withdrawal, silent suffering, jealousy.

In divorce cases, visits by the absent parent can cause further eruptions. Children often are caught in the bind of how to show affection for one parent without betraying the other. And neighbors frequently, to begin with, at least, become hypercritical of children in a home just split by divorce and tend to boss the children.

Social Life. Finding ways to meet people socially is another problem.

"I long so for social life, and especially to be able to talk with a man," another woman said. "Goodness knows, there's precious little time in the week left over for me, but even if I find a couple of hours where will I go?"

"The church is for families," the widow of a pastor declared, after a year of trying to fit into her church in the new role as a single. "The Sunday morning worship is for all, but beyond that?"

"I know," said another widow. "At our last congregational supper I was ushered to a table with a few other singles, 'way in the back of the room. It would have been much more fun sitting with the couples."

One widow shared how she had solved that problem. Once a month at least and often twice, she gives a dinner party to which she invites two couples and two single people. "We have a wonderful time," she said, "and often they invite me back in turn. It gives me an opportunity for male companionship without causing feeling on the part of the wife, because I am constantly inviting different couples." She smiled a bit ruefully. "It's almost impossible, I've discovered, for a widow or divorcee to have

104

a single close male friend. We have to find our close friendships with women."

Loneliness. But perhaps the most difficult of all problems is the never-ceasing loneliness.

After her divorce a woman fled to a large city to begin a new life. She took a room on the fourth floor of the Y, where other divorced women were and where it was quiet. "The walls were paper-thin," she recalled. "That first night I lay in bed and listened to a woman in the other room cry for two hours."

"I don't know what I'd do without my work," one new widow said. "But the toughest part of the day is coming home to an empty house."

"It's not just having someone with whom you can talk over problems," another said. "If the children are on their own and managing fine, as mine are, there aren't problems to face every day. But it's just not having someone with whom you can share all the happenings of the day—the small talk."

"And there's the restless longing inside for a mate," another confessed. "Someone you can love and give yourself to totally: emotionally, physically, intellectually. The old search is on again. I find myself looking, wondering . . . "

"I know," said another, "and I tell myself to be realistic and remember there are 43 million women over 40 and only 36 million men. But still I keep looking."

Widowed and Divorced Singles Can Cope

In spite of their problems, most widowed and divorced singles do learn to cope.

Mary's husband died when she was only 50. Mary was a registered nurse but hadn't worked for 25 years. But with a son to help through medical school Mary decided to go back to college to receive the training that would enable her to get a good job. She lived in a dorm and worked as head resident which provided a little extra income for her. Mary earned a degree in speech and hearing therapy, then went on to get her master's degree. "Sometimes the going was rough," her daughter admitted, "but she completed her studies, and we are very proud of her."

Sharon's husband walked out on her, leaving her three children to support. She began selling cosmetics, then took courses in developing poise and good grooming. Today her schedule is full as she gives lectures in public schools to girl scouts, airline stewardesses, and sales clerks in department stores.

Life lost meaning for Ruth when both her husband and only child were killed. Stunned, she could do nothing for months. Finally volunteer work among retarded children brought balm and healing. As her love for them grew, she determined to give the rest of her life for them. She enrolled in college taking special courses to help the retarded, received her degree in her fifties and taught for several years before her retirement.

Winsomely attractive Marilyn Hamilton, divorced with one child to care for, found self-pity draining away when she accepted an opportunity to serve. Marilyn tells about it in *Chatelaine:*

"I commuted every night to a farm twenty miles away. There in the kitchen of an extremely rundown shack I taught English to two Tibetan refugee couples and learned the greatest lesson of my life.

"These people had experienced communist terrorism, the loss of property and of wealth, the death of loved ones. They had had children die in their arms; hunger, disease and any other form of privation you might care to name they had experienced. They understood life at its primary level and they accepted it accordingly.

"Even though I taught sometimes with my coat and boots on, huddled in front of the one faulty gas heater that once tried to gas us, I went in every night with a grateful heart, for the serenity and love that was expressed in the homes of these Tibetan refugees.

"They were thankful to be in Canada, to be alive, to be together, and a bathroom out back in forty below weather seemed little enough sacrifice.

"Somehow my problems came to feel plastic, self-imposed and a foolish extravagance. I didn't need them. They could be dis-

106

regarded. I realize now how easy it is to worry over things in our society that are really not all that significant . . . I now teach full-time at the college here in Edmonton in a course called English for New Canadians, and am dedicated to the future of this program."

Those Who Have Never Married

The situation of those who have never married is unique in some respects.

The person who has never married is looked at askance. Society continues to insist marriage is the norm, though even statistically speaking, if monogamy is followed, marriage for all is impossible. Perhaps no one realizes this more clearly than the unmarried Christian girl.

Why is she unmarried? Some choose to remain single: to care for aging parents or a handicapped relative, to pursue advance study or a career that is either very demanding or calls for mobility. A few just enjoy the freedom of being single and don't want the responsibilities of marriage. A handful do not like children. But perhaps most are single simply because they do not meet someone they can love and who loves them.

Emotional Problems. The person who has never married may face unique emotional problems. As one expressed it: "During the middle years one begins, not only to face up to the fact that she is not married, but one also begins to find the reasons, in some cases, why she is not. This discovery is even more disturbing. Pride, self-protection, fears, invulnerability, among other things, have stood in the way, and I realize now that things might have been different."

Financial Problems. Even with income tax hitting him hard, the single man usually is better off financially than his married counterpart. Studies show, however, that single women often do not invest their savings in ways that could bring sizeable returns. They seem afraid to take risks. Thus when they arrive at the middle years, and retirement becomes imminent, they often become concerned as to whether or not they will have enough to care for themselves.

"Some mornings I wake up with a tight tension band around my head," the secretary to a vice president of a corporation said. Her employer had just retired. The man who had moved up to replace him brought with him his own secretary. The company was at a loss to know what to do with the secretary who had worked for them for over 25 years. "I go to work and stare at my face reflected in the polish of an empty desk," the secretary said. "They keep telling me there will be something for me. But will there? And what will it be? Will I be dropped to the basement? Farmed out? Invited to retire? Will they decide the retirement benefits I have accrued are going to be too costly for the company so they'll give me work so demeaning I'll resign of my own volition? I wonder about all this, and the band around my head gets tighter and tighter."

Difficulty in Achieving Independence. The single person who continues to live at home might discover after a while that he is not allowed to grow up. Although he may have younger brothers and sisters who are completely free, he may be treated like a child. One single complained his mother still tells him when to shampoo his hair, what shirt to wear, and even asks what time he will be home at night.

The girl who continues to live at home often does not realize all the implications at first. Her job absorbs her interest. She is content to have her own room and luxuriates in having all her needs cared for: house cleaned, meals cooked, laundry done. Often not until she has reached the middle years does discontent set in. Then she begins to wish she had a little home of her own or even an apartment where she could come and go at will and furnish as she would like. A friend tells her: "I come home from work dead tired. Often I lie down and sleep until 8:00. Then I awaken refreshed and prepare myself a good dinner and really enjoy my evening." The one at home, still fenced in by parents' routine feels envious. Resentment begins to smoulder. Tension builds up.

But would it be fair to ask the aging parents to adapt their way of life to hers? They have, after all, spent 20 or 30 years adjusting their lives, seeking the welfare of their children, although this is difficult for anyone not a parent to understand.

Resentments Which May Develop. The tension which develops becomes a wall, not only between the adult child and his aging parents, but between the single adult and God, preventing him from receiving all the help God has for him.

Even the single living on his own may experience resentment towards God—resentment because of having to carry life's load alone, of having to face the insecurity of retirement alone, of lying ill alone in his apartment, of not having normal sexual drives satisfied, of being the "child" expected to care for the aging parents.

The single is tempted to feel she is not desirable or wanted. (I say *she* simply because more women than men face the problem.) This, in turn, can produce inferiority feeling of worthlessness, of not liking or being able to accept one's self. Self-pity is at hand to smother one. It is only a step from there to bitterness, sarcasm, and a critical spirit. Having no one to whom it is necessary to defer, it becomes all too easy to become egocentric, thinking mainly of one's self, spending one's money on elaborate wardrobes or costly vacations. Rigidity can set in also so the slightest interruption of one's schedule can prove upsetting or the expression of another's point of view cannot be tolerated.

But there is a way out. First, the inner resentment towards God should be surrendered. One learns to accept his situation as from the hand of a loving Father and thank him for it. This calls for *faith*, because we cannot see all the factors God can. We have to believe he knows best.

We might have to make this declaration of faith and surrender over and over. It is difficult to be so decisive that temptations never come again, but following the initial surrender, subsequent relinquishments of our hold on our "rights" should be easier.

When our resentment has been brought to Christ, who will cleanse us from it, we can proceed.

We recognize we are not unique in having problems. Even married people do. It is helpful to sit down and list all we have going for us. All of us need to accept the fact that we may have to live with a certain amount of loneliness. But if we are single, we are free in ways married people are not. We can explore avenues of service open to us because we are single and mobile; we can be adventuresome and we can choose almost any career we wish.

Developing a positive, thankful attitude helps. Finding a substitute family enriches our lives. Even our avocations can be turned outward to benefit others. We can cultivate new friends, of different social status and race and backgrounds, and as we do, in a few instances, we might even find a mate. For nothing attracts another as much as a person who is vibrantly alive and happy. Not that finding a mate need be the goal necessarily. Single life can be complete and intensely rewarding and interesting.

Many Unmarried Persons Live Rich Lives

We all know singles who have transformed small houses or apartments into attractive homes reflecting the personality of the person living there, singles who unselfishly have shared their lives with their extended families and become favorite aunts and uncles, singles who live beautiful, purposeful, satisfying lives. Many pastors can testify to dedicated, faithful service given by the singles within the congregation. One friend of mine, who has been active in youth work, has had the joy of helping over 100 come to faith in Jesus Christ. And what would have happened to the advance and growth of Christ's church overseas without all the single missionaries? Our saying there was: "The woman is the man to do the job!" One wonders sometimes, would the lives of these singles have been as fruitful if marriage had placed its restraints on them?

How the Church Can Help

What can married people do to stretch out a hand of friendship to the singles to draw them into the circle of the church's family from which they often feel they are outcasts?

110

Garden Grove Community Church in Garden Grove, California, has been asking itself this question. In 1974 they called a pastor specifically to this ministry. He gives full attention to developing the "Positive Christian Singles" group, composed of over 300 divided into The Seekers, The Pacesetters, The Innovators, The Motivators, and The Lamplighters. A bright orange brochure winsomely outlines their programs. For example, the Motivators introduce themselves: "The Motivators are Positive Christian Singles in their 40s who come together on Sunday mornings to share in Bible study and spiritual inspiration. The motto of our class is 'We Care.' We meet on Sunday mornings at 9:30 on the sixth floor of the tower to learn more on how God can be the answer to our problems. At the close of class time you will be given a calendar of events and an invitation to join us in a local restaurant for lunch. On Tuesday evenings we have an informal get-together where everyone can feel free to discuss our everyday problems, our feelings and beliefs and our joys. Saturday nights we have our socials which include potlucks, theater parties, and various other recreational activities. We attend the 11:15 service and the evening service at 7:00 P.M. Feel free to come and worship with your Motivator friends. You will find us on the left side of the sanctuary about halfway down."

The groups each have a Now-Help Committee with a chairman who steers those with the know-how to homes plagued with leaky faucets or plugged drains. The group depends on its own manpower. It does not call on help from married couples. More than one-third of the group are actively involved in some area of service in the church. A Youth Partners program, patterned after the Big Brother program, provides a father or mother figure for the child deprived of one or the other.

"But we believe," Kenneth Van Wyck, minister of Christian Education stated, "that the needs of the singles are best met on a spiritual basis. Introducing them to Jesus Christ and nourishing their Christian faith is the most significant contribution we can make. This is the peculiar role of the church. We must keep the groups redemptive. They must not become just another club.

"Any church which seeks to minister to singles in its congregation and community," Pastor Van Wyck assured me, "will receive gratitude and unbounded love. There are no more appreciative people than singles who have been helped."

Small churches usually find they can minister best by initiating joint programs with other local churches.

A few singles resent any "singling out." "I belong to a small church," one said. "I'm happy there. I count. I'm accepted. I'm not considered odd, but just one of them." This, undoubtedly, is the ideal.

Many family counselors have expressed the wish that more families would include singles in their family circle.

"It calls for a rare married woman," one divorcee said almost bitterly. "My experience has been that soon after I become friends with a couple, the woman begins to eye me with suspicion. I represent a threat."

Singles, as well as married people, need to pause midway in life to consider their goals, examine them to see if they are worthy, and then set for themselves reasonable goals. Working towards definite goals can be one of the best substitutes for sex, and it trims loneliness to a tolerable level.

Hopefully, this chapter also has pulled back the curtain a little and let married people look in briefly on what life is like for a single. All too often, we walk around with stereotyped mental pictures. Perhaps as the married person sets new goals for the second half of his life, one of them can be related to loving the singles.

Books of Interest

Woman Alone by Evelyn King Mumaw
The Single Woman by Ruth Reed
A Woman Doctor Looks at Life and Love by Marion Hillyard
Try Giving Yourself Away by David Dunn
The Single Girl's Guide to Living in the City by Gwen Cummings
The Church and the Single Person by Frances M. Bontrager
Facing Life Alone by Marian Champagne

Parents Without Partners by Jim Egleson and Janet F. Egleson
After Divorce by William Goode
Raising Your Child in a Fatherless Home by Eve Jones
To Live Again by Catherine Marshall
When You're a Widow by Clarissa Start
The Single Adult and the Church by Elmer L. Towns
The One-Parent Family by Anna W. M. Wolf and Lucille Stein
For the Love of Singles by Sarah Jepson

9

The Search for Security

*Final security is a matter of faith. It is
what we believe about ourselves, our fellow men, about the purpose of life, about
God that determines our deepest security.*
—LOWELL RUSSELL DITZEN

Ask six of your friends what their chief concerns are mid-stream
in life and all six will put security near the top of the list. But
chances are they will also mention the need to do something different, in order to get rid of the "blahs" in their life. At the same
time, while they might not refer to it, the burden of assuming
responsibility for a million different things actually is consuming
most of their time.

Are these three needs: the need for security, the need for adventure, and the need for assuming responsibility actually opposed to each other? Not really. In fact, handled aright they can
fit together like pieces of a puzzle.

True, our need for adventure may be stifled because of our
fear of taking risks. But understanding wherein true security lies
actually will enable us to take risks. And adventure becomes most
satisfying when it is linked with our need to assume responsibility.
So the following chapters form a trilogy. They are closely related
to each other, and all concern themselves with how we can
satisfy in meaningful and valid ways three of our basic human
needs: the need for security, adventure, and assuming responsibility.

It is important that we satisfy these needs aright. Unmet needs
give birth to frustration, dissatisfaction, irritability, and com-

plaining and can cripple us from growing and developing as persons.

Let's think, first of all, of the need for security. How do we often attempt to answer our need for security? To what do we turn?

Loyal Mates

We all want the security that comes with knowing our mate loves us.

A young man in one of the college classes I attended told me one day: "My father and mother were separated for a while. Now they are together again, but Dad is so afraid he'll do something to upset Mom he's all tied up in knots. He told me last night the tension was getting almost unbearable, and he didn't know how much longer he could stand it."

That husband is not secure in his relationship with his wife. How different the words of George Eliot in "The Essence of Friendship": "Oh, the comfort, the inexpressible comfort of feeling safe with a person, having neither to weigh nor measure words, but to pour them all out, just as they are, chaff and grain together, knowing that a faithful hand will take and sift them, keep what is worth keeping, and then, with the breath of kindness blow the rest away."

Many read that wistfully and wish that were true of their married life. With steadily rising divorce rates, some wonder uneasily if it will happen to them next.

Friends

Knowing we have loved ones, relatives and friends, to whom we can turn at a time of need does bring a sense of security. We can face almost anything if we know we won't have to face it alone.

A friend whose son was born blind tells of the dark despair that engulfed her for months after their doctor told them there was nothing he could do. The first glimmer of hope came when a friend took her to a meeting of parents of other blind children. She listened with awe as she heard them plan activities for their children. A little while later she enrolled for Braille classes, so she would be able to help her son when he began school. "To my surprise," she says, "I found few parents in the class, but many who were just interested in helping blind children. I had had no idea so many cared. I was overwhelmed. Suddenly I didn't feel alone any more. I felt I could face the future with confidence. It marked a real turning point for me."

But even good friends might forsake us. There is as much treason in the world as friendship. The disciples left Jesus and fled. It is very unlikely we shall be able to go through life without being betrayed by some friends. So while we do well to cultivate and nourish friendships, still our ultimate hope for security cannot rest with our friends.

Self-esteem

Some of us might still be seeing the security that comes from an assurance of self-worth.

When my husband was pastor in Canada, he was called upon to officiate at the funeral of a man who had lived a hermit existence in a shack in the back woods. There was no one to mourn his death, absolutely no one, so completely had he lived apart from people.

Why had this man withdrawn so completely? His secret remains locked within him. We can only speculate. Was he so unsure of himself and so fearful of what lay out in the world that his only security was in withdrawal? How different it could have been if he had been able to see himself as a person created and loved by God and therefore as a person of infinite worth. This would have made him strong and enabled him to take his place in the world as a contributing member. Happy the person who develops self-assurance early in life, but thank God, it never is too late.

Developed Skills and Robust Health

Developing and perfecting new skills is one way to cultivate self-confidence.

A man who had experienced periodic spells of being laid off approached me on the church patio one Sunday morning with a beaming face. "Brighter days should be ahead for us," he said. "Wife and I talked over our situation. We thought about what each of us enjoyed doing most. We asked ourselves if job opportunities in those fields were plentiful right across the nation. After investigation we decided they were. So we took time out, and both of us got some specialized training. Now we're both working, both enjoying our work and both reasonably sure we shall be able to get a job wherever we go. It's a good feeling."

Their decision had been wise, but to put all one's trust in one's own cleverness or ability is hardly safe. A few months later this man's wife became ill with a lingering, baffling disease. The family lost half their source of income and even with the help of medical insurance, bills mounted. Once again this family felt acutely the need for financial security.

Financial Security

The person in the middle years is very aware of the need for financial security. His only problem is that, although he knows he should save both for post-retirement needs and emergencies, what with mortgage payments, orthodontist bills, college tuition, and the ever-rising cost of living he never seems able to save— at least not as much as he would like. To cheer himself up, he rationalizes that he should have at least ten good earning years after the children are on their own, when he should be able to save. And aren't life insurance policies, real estate and pension plans savings? And yet he wishes he could save more.

Being Knowledgeable About Financial Affairs

We also need the security that comes with knowing how to care for the financial affairs of our family. Wives and husbands should be equally knowledgeable.

118

The husband of a friend of mine dropped dead at work one day. He had cared for all the business transactions of the family. His widow didn't know how to write even a check. Her confusion added to her already troubled state of mind. "If only," she lamented, "we had taken time to sit down and get all the information together in one book in a way I could understand."

If I am having trouble living within my salary, here are some questions to consider:

1. Am I spending too much on housing?
2. Do I have too many cars or too-expensive-to-operate cars?
3. Do I feel compelled to keep up with others?
4. Does my generous expense account at work make me tend to overspend at home?
5. Does my hobby cost more than it should?
6. Are we spending too much on clothes? on the kids?
7. Are we impulse buyers?
8. Do we buy depreciable items on credit?
9. Do we pay our bills promptly?
10. Do we keep record so we know where our money is going?
11. Do we tithe?

Other questions for consideration: Have we made adequate provision for our family in case of death? Have we made wills? Are they up-to-date? Stationery and book stores sell books where we can enter all the information our family should have if we die. Have we a record like this? Are both husband and wife knowledgeable in regard to financial affairs? Does our family know our wishes in regard to funeral and burial arrangements? Do we take reasonable precautions in regard to safeguarding our home against burglary and fire? Do we have lists of our furnishings or pictures of the rooms of our house?

True Security

What *does* make us feel secure? A loyal mate? Trusted friends? Health? A steady job? A pocket full of skills to draw from? A stable government? A reliable law enforcement system? Insur-

119

ance policies? Justice in the courts? Hospitalization insurance? Retirement funds? Savings?

But what if all these should crumble? It happened to Job. It has happened to others since. It could happen to us. Wherein would our security lie then?

This is when we need the security we find when we are rightly related to God. Webster's dictionary defines security as "safety, protection, freedom from uncertainty or doubt." But it also defines it as "the condition of being firmly fastened or secured." The man who is fastened to the Lord will be secure. He knows God will meet his needs.

"My savings have shrunk, and my monthly income is small," an 84-year-old single lady told me. "But the Lord looks after me. Two years ago I felt prompted to increase my hospitalization insurance. I didn't know at the time that the next two years would bring heavy medical expenses. I went blind for a while. The doctor thought I would never see again. But I don't have resources to pay someone to care for all my needs. So I prayed, and the Lord restored enough vision so I can take care of myself. I needed a new coat and shoes and my watch had broken. On my birthday I received some cash gifts. I went down and found both the coat and shoes on sale and had enough left to buy a watch. So, you see," she said contentedly, "the Lord takes care of his own. It's like the Psalmist said, 'I have been young and now am old, but I have not seen God's people begging bread.' "

The serene faith and trust of this old saint reflects the spirit Jesus wanted to see in his followers when he said, "Be not anxious." In today's language Jesus probably would say, "Don't come apart, don't go to pieces." The man secure in God does not come apart when faced with need—any need. He knows God will take care of him. The certainty that he is being upheld by God strengthens him, weak though he may feel. In the end, this is the assurance we need most.

A Minnesota farmer, father of five, awakened one night with severe pain in his shoulder. Within 24 hours his right arm dangled useless at his side. Several weeks later the doctors at Mayo

120

Clinic diagnosed his trouble as acute bilateral brachial plexitis, a rare nerve disease. The doctors were dubious as to whether he would ever regain the use of his arms.

"The day they broke that news to us it was gray and raining," his wife said. "We walked back to our motel room. I picked up my Bible and a tract tumbled out. I read these words of F. B. Meyer: 'Never act in panic . . . wait upon God until he makes known his way. He accounts himself responsible for all the results of keeping thee where thou art.'

"If God is willing to assume responsibility for what has happened to us, we can trust him," the wife said. They committed themselves to God.

"I think the fact I was a farmer made it easier also for me to accept what had happened in an attitude of trust," Oscar said many months later when he had regained the use of his right arm and partial use of his left one. "Rain—too much or too little —storms, sickness in the herd, blight, pests, hail—all have taught me to accept disappointments, failures, illnesses, and set-backs and carry on patiently. All of these I consider only as opportunities to grow in faith and trust in God. Thus during my illness, though at times I felt frustrated, I never felt licked. We never doubted that God would see us through. The lines of an old hymn kept coming back: 'His love in times past forbids me to think / He'll leave me at last in trouble to sink.' "

So for the Christian, security does not mean being shielded or saved from danger, risk, or evil. Rather it means knowing God is with us, regardless what comes. "In the world you *will have* tribulation," Jesus assured his followers, and then added, "but be of good cheer! I have overcome the world." Jesus is with us. This assurance will see us through.

In Britain during World War II when the cities were being bombed, hundreds of the children were sent to homes in the country where they would be cared for and safe. But a few parents chose to keep their children with them. Surprisingly enough, the children who had their parents with them, though they were exposed to danger, survived better than those who lived in safety, but separated from their parents.

121

The man who is convinced God is with him, that God will never abandon him, is truly secure. With this security comes courage. With this security and courage we can face the future with confidence and calmness. We will find strength to be true to our convictions even when we are challenged and opposed. We will not hesitate to act when we are convinced what we are doing is right. We even will be enabled to take risks that are necessary to respond to the call of duty.

"We are pressed on every side by trouble," Paul wrote to the Corinthians, "but not crushed and broken. We are perplexed because we don't know why things happen as they do, but we don't give up and quit. We are hunted down, but God never abandons us. We get knocked down, but we get up again and keep going. These bodies of ours are constantly facing death just as Jesus did; so it is clear to all that it is only the living Christ within [who keeps us safe]." (2 Corinthians 4:8-10. Living Bible).

Thus secure in our God, as we assume the responsibilities we should in mid-life, our need for adventure will be satisfied in the right way. It is this need we shall discuss next.

10

Forever Explorers at Heart

> *It is dangerous to have one's golden age behind one. It is the opposite of adventure. Life is a one-way street.*
>
> —PAUL TOURNIER

All of us, from time to time, get bored with our day to day and year to year routine and long for a new adventure. The person in his middle years often feels the need acutely. To date he perhaps has met it by steadily advancing in his job. But now he has peaked out. The adventure of advancement is dead, but he is still chained to his job.

"I'm afraid I'm a bit envious of my wife," one man said. "She went to work a few years ago when our children no longer needed all her attention, and a whole new world opened to her. But myself . . . I just looked forward to work and then more work." He felt his days of adventure and exploration were behind him, that the 9–5 grind was all that remained for him.

Some Satisfy the Need for Adventure in the Wrong Way

It is important that we find right ways of satisfying our need for adventure, for if the need is not met, frustration and boredom set in. Then the drive for adventure can become so compelling it may lead us to satisfying it in wrong ways. Quite possibly this accounts for the frequent extra-marital affairs so common in middle age. Usually these are engaged in for "kicks" only, not because the men and women have any serious intent to enter into a new, permanent relationship.

Becoming completely absorbed in outside activities is another way in which some seek to satisfy the need for adventure. Gaugin, at 45, abandoned a successful banking career and his family and want to Tahiti to paint. During these days of liberating forces at work, some women, glorying in their new-found liberty when the children get older, become so caught up with and fascinated by their jobs or the education they are acquiring that they turn their back on family responsibilities. Some even run away, and in doing so overlook yet another need they have: the need for assuming responsibility.

Some Satisfy the Need for Adventure in Second-hand Ways

Many seek satisfaction in second-hand ways. They read adventure stories or go to the movies or watch TV. Recently, when I attended a ball game with our son, I saw a middle-aged man become the self-appointed cheer leader of his section of spectators. Turning to face the spectators, he gesticulated wildly, jumping up and down, causing the beer in the can he was grasping to fountain out and be spilled. He shouted to the fans to give all they had to their cheers and boos. He was out to get his adventure in a big way.

Others feverishly campaign for their political favorite, and after the election proudly proclaim, "We won." Some get their adventure by day-dreaming or fantasizing. Some rehearse their adventures of earlier years. Others wander from one amusement park to another. Braver ones venture out and they themselves try soaring or roaring across fields in the winter in snowmobiles or shooting rapids in canoes. Or have you ever noticed the number of older men zooming around in expensive, high-powered, low-slung sports cars?

Satisfying the Need for Adventure in Meaningful Ways

The need for adventure cries out for satisfaction whether or not people are aware of it being a need of theirs. How can we satisfy it in meaningful and productive ways?

We can develop new skills. There are many fields to explore.

Robert Frost had been farming in New Hampshire and teaching in prep schools. But his restlessness grew until finally he sold all and went to England. There on his small farm he began to write poems. His first poem was published when he was 40.

Pearl Buck was just about 40 when her first novel, *East Wind, West Wind* was published. She went on to win the Pulitzer Prize and the Nobel Prize and wound up writing almost 70 books!

George Bernard Shaw's literary career began after he was 40.

Have you always wanted to write? Catherine Marshall suggests six characteristics of a writer:

1. Did you dream of writing when you were little?
2. Do you love to write? Would you write without reward?
3. Is solitude one of your natural habitats?
4. Do you continually see stories in life, in yourself, in others around you?
5. Do you have an innate story sense? Do you love a story?
6. Does the recording of life's events seem important to you? Are you saying to other people, "Put it down"?

Perhaps your skills, discovered or undiscovered, lie in weaving, woodwork, ceramics, leather or metal craft, mosaics, sewing, mechanics, photography, gardening, cooking.

Walter Knott of Knott's Berry Farm in Buena Park, California, which grosses 15 million dollars annually, left his farm in the Mojave Desert where he couldn't make enough to support four children and moved to Buena Park. He was past 40 at the time, but he took out a loan so he could buy a 10-acre farm where he raised boysenberries to sell at a roadstand. Mrs. Knott began to make berry pies and biscuits. People clamored for them. Encouraged, Mrs. Knott began to serve chicken dinners. Attractions were added: myna birds, an exhibit of candy making. Little by little, imagination and hard work transformed the 10 acres into one of the most famous recreation centers in California.

Mrs. Ruby Omvig, postmistress of Mylo, North Dakota, uses her evenings to make quilts for destitute people the world over. She puts together a quilt a week. "I feel making quilts is one of the tasks God has assigned me, and the fact that I truly enjoy it is an added bonus," says Mrs. Omvig. She buys most of the material at rummage sales and thrift shops, where she looks for extra full skirts and draperies.

Or does political service appeal to you? Harry S. Truman's haberdashery business collapsed when he was 40. He ran for and was elected county judge. Although he had only a high school education, he ran for the U.S. Senate when he was 60, and at 61 he succeeded Roosevelt as president. At 64 he won the office in his own right.

If you like to travel, you can go places you have never been before. If you have worked long enough to earn a sizeable chunk of vacation time, consider swapping homes during your vacation and going places where otherwise you maybe couldn't afford to go. Vacation Exchange Club, 663 Fifth Avenue, New York, 10022, publishes a directory of its 5000 members (30% of them outside the U.S.). You can list your name, house description, and desired time and place for the swap. Then you're on your own; you do your own correspondence; there is no screening or no guarantee. There are also bureaus that for a fee will make arrangements, investigate character and credit of anyone using this service. Check with your travel agent.

If you love to learn, you can enroll in a continuing adult education class, construct your family's genealogy, engage in research, make the acquaintance of people by reading their biographies, attend classes at a Bible school or seminary, write your family history.

If health is good, *take up a new sport:* golf, fishing, flying, boating, camping, bowling, hiking.

If you are confined to the armchair, get your adventure through TV, radio, stereo. Invite in friends. Teach a class in your home. Try some adventures in thinking. Dare to read books you haven't before. Play tapes. Listen to the points of view of people who differ from you.

If you are temporarily unemployed, develop an idea you have been tossing around in your mind for a long time. Charles Darrow at 45 lost his job. Whiling away his time at home, he invented Monopoly. The middle years' love of comfort motivated Anton Lorenz, a teacher of history and geography in Hungary, to design the Barcalounger Reclining Chair. Over two million have been sold. Castro wanted both beauty and comfort. He designed his first graceful looking sofa bed when he was 43.

Trusting the Lord to give you victory in areas where you have often suffered defeat can be an adventure. It's a great feeling to master a mood or habit that has been controlling you. Even taking off excess pounds can be an adventure.

Sometimes adventure comes as a person begins a new work. By the time he is 40, if not earlier, a person should know whether or not his work is satisfying enough for him to want to continue at it for another 25 years. If it isn't, he is well advised to make a change.

"Worse than illness," Dr. Thomas Holmes, University of Washington professor of psychiatry, states, "is to go on in an intolerable, dull, or demeaning situation."

Albert Schweitzer was almost 40 when he arrived in Africa. When someone questioned his move, he replied, "I consider myself too blessed and feel called to bring a candle of learning to the darkness."

Usually, however, one does not change vocations mid-stream in life. But *discovering innovative methods to use in one's own work can bring freshness to an old job and zest to living.* Sometimes *a change in attitude* toward our work may be all that is needed. We need to be convinced our job is important, that even though we work with things, still the things we produce benefit and serve people. Or we can discover a ministry among those with whom we work.

One of our sons worked for a while as errand boy for a large savings and loan company. Some of his friends, who had worked there previously, had quickly tired of the monotony and felt the job held little challenge. Dan's response was: "I don't mind the work. When I deliver the mail or run errands, I try to see the people to whom I make the delivery. Many of them are so uptight. The business world is tough. Those above can make it really rough for the guy below. When I see their worried looks, I smile, pat them on the back and tell them things will work out some-how and that God loves them and cares."

When we view our jobs as our vocation from God, even menial tasks glow. "There can be no work," Calvin declared, "however vile or sordid that does not glisten before God, and is not right precious, provided that in it we serve our vocation. . . . Every man . . . in his place ought to dream that his estate is, as it were, a station assigned to him by God."

Brother Lawrence, the long-ago author of *Practising the Presence of God,* washed pots and pans and rubbed and scoured and polished their bottoms so every pan became a beaming, happy face, and the presence of God filled the rectory kitchen.

E. Stanley Jones at his *ashrams* in India used to demonstrate by example the nobility of *all* work. Participants at the ashrams used to sign up for various household chores. Jones frequently chose to empty the wastebuckets from the latrines.

Many find new zest and interest in life as they plunge into volunteer work. Volunteer work first provided adventure and then later opened the door to an ever-enlarging ministry for Beverly Petersen of Van Nuys, California. Beverly tells her story:

"When I answered the telephone on a Monday afternoon in early November, 1960, I had no idea that this was the beginning of my adventure in saying 'yes!' The Director of Volunteers of Pacoima Memorial Lutheran Hospital was calling. 'Could I give four hours a week to work at the hospital?' she asked. My children were in school. Why not?

"I was assigned to the Director of Nursing Services and found myself engulfed in making stencils for nursing procedures, running the mimeograph and assembling manuals. As I typed, I sometimes saw ideas that could be clarified by re-statement. I made suggestions. Often my revision would show up in the final copy. I sought to become more useful.

"For eight years I worked at the hospital. During this period I said 'yes' again when asked if I would stand for nomination as a district assembly chairperson of the Lutheran Church Women of the Pacific Southwest Synod of the Lutheran Church in America. That 'yes' was the door opening to many wonderful friendships. Visits and letters from others widened my horizons. Opportunities for leadership training presented themselves also. Soon I was conducting dozens of one-day workshops. Although I suffered from butterflies in my stomach at the beginning of each workshop, before it was over I found I was enjoying what I was doing.

"After each workshop I carefully reviewed the written evaluations prepared by the workshop participants, being appreciative of the constructive criticisms and encouraged by the compliments as I sought to improve the next presentation.

"Soon I was serving on the synodical unit executive board of LCW. This brought more training experience, opportunities to participate in program planning and to help develop and write materials for workshop presentations.

"Our children were now approaching college age. We needed to supplement our family income. So it seemed like an answer to our need when Rev. John C. Simmons, hospital administrator of Golden State Community Mental Health Center, asked if I would be interested in a position as administrative assistant. I laughed. 'Everything I know about the mental health field you can put in a thimble and still have room left over for your finger,' I said to him.

"Rev. Simmons explained that my primary responsibility would be to work towards developing better communication and working relationships between various departments and personnel. A catalyst between people? A mediator? I wondered if I could be effective in this new role. The administrator seemed to think so. So again I said, 'yes.'

"My latest adventure began July, 1971. Dr. Carl W. Segerhammar, President of the Pacific Southwest Synod of the Lutheran Church in America, called to say I had been elected by the Synod Executive Board as a member of the board to fill a vacant, unexpired term. I would be, he stated, the first woman in this synod to serve in such a capacity. Would I accept? Just being 'first' made my knees weak.

"Almost immediately after my election was announced several younger women contacted me, asking for support in focusing on the role of women in the church. As a result a forum on women was held at the next synod convention. Ninety-six persons attended. Only four were men!

"While a part of the board I tried to point out the anti-women attitudes which sometimes were reflected in speech and points of view. Sometimes the sessions were emotionally quite difficult for me, because we were examining traditional concepts and contemplating change. Many of us were already part of this change; others of us were just beginning to become aware of it.

"Looking back over the years, I can see how each experience was a preparation for the next, helping me develop the abilities and self-confidence which I would need for the next adventure. 'Stick-to-it-tiveness,' I have discovered, goes a long way. Education and training often can be gained on the job. In addition, I use every opportunity I can to take college courses and attend seminars.

"Saying 'yes' has broadened my horizons. I shall always be glad I accepted challenge. Of course one does not venture out like this alone. My husband and family were always ready to give a word of encouragement. When things got tough, I was conscious of God always being by my side, assuring me of his help. And that means most to me, for more than anything else I want to be his witness in my work."

"The tragedy of life is not so much what men suffer as what they miss," Thomas Carlyle affirmed.

The need for adventure continues to be a basic need of man throughout his life. Man is an explorer at heart. True satisfaction of his need will come, not through exploration in fields that are morally out-of-bounds, but in response to the rightful demands society places on him; not in passively viewing the adventures of others, but by his own plunging into ventures; not even in development of innate gifts solely for the joy and satisfaction of development, but in using those gifts to serve the larger community.

Jesus still calls us to adventure with him. The words in which he clothes his invitation may sound strange to our ears, but deep within ourselves we know he is speaking the truth. We feel the tug at our hearts and want to respond.

He declares: "Unless a grain of wheat falls into the earth and dies, it remains alone; but if it dies, it bears much fruit. He who loves his life loses it, and he who hates his life in this world will keep it for eternal life. If any one serves me, he must follow me; and where I am, there shall my servant be also" (John 12:24-26).

If we will let God lead us, he will take us down new roads and open new vistas. All other adventures will pale before the great adventure of following Jesus as Lord. Just when we thought life was becoming dull and commonplace, we shall discover instead that it throbs with new, unexpected surprises, a promise of the best yet to come.

Books About New Perspectives for Women

The Potential of Women: An Interdisciplinary Approach edited by Seymour Farber and Roger Wilson

Developing Women's Potential by Edwin C. Lewis

380 Part-Time Jobs for Women by Ruth Lembeck

Creative Careers for Women: A Handbook of Sources and Ideas for Part-Time Jobs by Joan Scobey and Lee P. McGrath

Women in American Politics by Martin Gruberg

Few Are Chosen: American Women in Political Life Today by Peggy Lamson

11

The Road Leads Uphill All the Way

Does the road lead uphill all the way?
All the way, my friend.
Does the journey last the livelong day?
From morn to night, my friend.

Shakespeare categorized the seven stages of man in this way: infants, school children, lovers, soldiers, travelers, leaders in development, and then, significantly, defines man's last span of life as being one where he is guardian of the soul of the nation.

Our Responsibility Defined

Guardian of the soul of the nation—an awesome responsibility, calling for the preservation and propagation of the noble and worthy principles on which our country was founded. For Christians the phrase suggests another unique responsibility: concern for our own relationship to God and also the relationship of others to God.

For even as Christians are concerned about the hurts, ills, injustices, and problems of this present world, they believe also that life does not end with the grave. They believe that the quality of the life we will have after the resurrection will be determined here and now, by our attitudes toward God and all God has to offer. Because of this Christians see themselves and all others of double value: because of the humans they are now and because of what they will become. The Christian is concerned about *both*.

How Are We Handling Responsibility in Our Middle Years?

Those in the middle years have been described by *Time* magazine as "The Command Generation." That is, we make the decisions, we carry the major portion of responsibilities. How are we doing the job?

1. *Some shirk responsibility.* They assume as little responsibility as possible. When confronted with larger needs, they have many reasons for not becoming involved. Let us consider some of the reasons given and ask if they are valid.

"I'm not responsible for the problems that exist; it's not my fault."

"Middle-agers are like Mexican burros," an article in *Changing Times* stated. "They carry an incredible load and receive a good many kicks to boot."

Many feel this way. As they see it, they are paying heavy taxes and doling out a major share of college expenses and then are accused of being slaves to a work ethic. They have worked for better living conditions, provided medical care for their families, contributed to medical research, and have had families half or even a fourth the size of their predecessors, yet they are told they have caused the overpopulation of the world by having all the kids they did. They provide comfortably for their families and are told their affluent living has brought on the ecological crisis. They are children or grandchildren or even great-grandchildren of immigrants, yet they are blamed for all the injustices done to the Blacks, the Indians, the Chicanos, the Migrant Workers.

"I've had it—up to here!" said one, drawing a swift line under his chin. "If I hear one more word about Indians, I'll punch someone in the nose."

"I refuse, I absolutely refuse to feel guilty about problems which have their roots in another century," another said heatedly.

Because of all the accusations hurled at them, many in their middle years feel unappreciated, misunderstood, and unduly blamed for problems they alone did not cause. Their reaction is to withdraw.

134

But can we say we are not guilty? Even though we personally may not be responsible for the major world problems that exist, still because we are members of the human race, are we not corporately guilty?

This does not mean we have to be weighed down with guilt. We make clear our penitence by doing what we can to correct the wrong that has been done, and we accept God's forgiveness. But we acknowledge our guilt, our anger, and our bias to ourselves and to others; we do not defensively deny it.

"Why should I contribute? Funds are mishandled."

"India? Why should I be concerned about India's poverty when I learn how much they squander on nuclear weapons? And so what if people there are dying of hunger? Thank God a few are dying, or we'd all soon be dead."

And so in many cases cynicism and disillusionment are hatching lethargy, indifference, callousness, or resignation.

But as Christians are we not sons of One who causes the sun to shine on the just and the unjust? Do we not follow One who contributed to a corruption-ridden priesthood system at the same time as he worked for reform? Do we not benefit daily from the gifts God pours out on us, whether we deserve them or not—or misuse them? And do not enough reliable agencies exist so we can channel our help through them?

"I've done my part."

Or we may hear: "Of course, I'm concerned. But we've worked hard and done our part. Someone else can take over now. It's only fair we should get to enjoy ourselves now. Fishing, boating, camping, travelling. We haven't had a chance to do this before. What's wrong with that?"

And so the route to self-indulgence is taken.

We need to ask ourselves if our resources are ours to use for selfish purposes or are they a trust gifted to us by God to be shared with those less fortunate than us? Is wealth a reward or a responsibility? Is it entrusted to us to provide security for us or is it given us as a tool to be used? And can we be truly happy just "doing what I've always wanted to do" when it reflects a life turned in upon itself? In time won't travel become commonplace, fishing monotonous, camping a chore? Won't the highest in us begin to stir up restless longings and dissatisfactions so we desire to do something purposeful again?

Dag Hammarskjold entered in his diary this word to himself: "You have not done enough, you have never done enough, so long as it is still possible that you have something of value to contribute."

Justice Holmes extended the age of assuming responsibility when on his 90th birthday he remarked: "The riders in a race do not stop short when they reach the goal. There is a little finishing canter before coming to a standstill. There is time to hear the kind voices of friends and to say to one's self, 'The work is done.' But just as one says that, the answer comes: 'The race is over, but the work is never done while the power to work remains.' To live is to function. That is all there is to living."

"The problem is too complicated for me; I wouldn't know what to do."

Some problems seem so gigantic, so snarled, so hopeless that our reaction may be to push a button and tune out that which disturbs us so greatly.

Famine. Disease. Intense social unrest. Violence. War. The seeds have sprouted. The crisis overhangs the world. It is not being faced realistically, and perhaps one reason is because it scares us to death to do so!

So, in defense, we rationalize. We say other people could make it like we did if they only would try. We declare there *are* enough world resources for all of us to live as comfortably as we do.

Or we try to escape by consoling ourselves with the thought that all these are but signs of the end times, that Jesus is coming soon, and then all our troubles will be over.

To look for the return of the Lord Jesus *is* the Christian's joyous, sustaining hope, but Christ never meant that expectancy to be the fire escape we take from the burning building. He wants us to be fire-fighters, not escapees.

Or we leave the problem to someone else to solve—who, we don't know specifically, but someone—there must be someone.

136

The fact is the problems are so enormous that to solve them calls for the accumulated, extensive experience of the most astute minds of the world and for the willingness to cooperate on the part of people, each of us, where we are, doing what we *can* do. To shirk this responsibility, to leave the solutions to our children, would be not only cruel, but immoral.

2. *Some do not support their stated priorities by the actual way in which they expend time, energy, and resources.*

How are we handling responsibility in our middle years? Some of us, with our lips, declare ourselves responsible for certain areas, but our lives do not support our declarations. We are living double lives. We rate high on our priority list a good marriage and a happy home, yet actually we give very little time, thought or effort to bringing this about. Loyalty to family and loyalty to job or career tears us apart. We respond most often to the one that brings in the money, and then feel guilty because we do so.

Again we try to rationalize our way out saying it is not the *quantity* of time that we give, but the *quality* that is important, forgetting that rarely can we have quality without quantity. The great works of art which have endured down through the years, the paintings, the sculpture, the literature, the music masterpieces, all have demanded enormous investments of time.

Also, the very fact that we have limited time often erodes the quality of that very time. Take, for example, the working parents' relationship to their children. Harried and overburdened with responsibilities both within and without the home, the little time they do spend with their family is often characterized by tension, pressure, haste, worry, and often short-temperedness. This is not always the case, of course. Some seem to thrive on huge loads of responsibility and rise to it and actually become better individuals. But in many cases a limited amount of time to give to the family also means a lower quality in the personal relationship extended during that time also.

We need to ask ourselves if our use of our time and energy truly reflects our priorities. If we don't bring these into line, we shall walk around unhappy because of the guilt we feel continually, and we also may respond in unappropriate ways to those we feel we are doing wrong to. For example, we may give our children extravagant allowances or spend excessive amounts to provide elaborate wardrobes for them or to allow them to participate in every activity their schools offer—regardless of cost. We substitute to salve our conscience, but our conscience refuses to let us be truly happy as long as we live double lives. We need to know who we are, what our values and responsibilities are, and then practice what we preach.

3. Some experience conflict between responsibility to themselves as persons as over against responsibility to others.

I heard the other day of a man in his 30s who studied first to become a minister. But he was not the kind of a minister his mother had hoped he would be. So he became a youth worker in a large church. But he was not the success at being a youth worker his mother had expected he would be. Now he is raising cacti. "On the front and back of my sweat shirt I have two signs which only I can read," the young man confessed. "One reads: 'How am I doing, Ma?' and the other one says, 'I'm really trying, Ma.'"

Some arrive at their middle years still caught in the bind of trying to be someone other than what they are. A distorted sense of responsibility to others imprisons them, forcing them to try to fit into roles that are repulsive to them. They have never promised themselves—and then acted on that promise—that first and foremost they will be true to themselves.

Even those who are trying to live out lives that reflect the "really, really me," need to continue to be aware of the need of assuming responsibility for ourselves. This might mean as simple an act as feeling free to take one day a week off for our own personal recreation, renewal, and refreshment. It might mean spending money to enrich and enhance our own inner lives instead of heaping all the privileges on our children. When Jesus commanded us to love our neighbors as ourselves, he was not scorning the importance of self-love, but rather underlining it. In order to act responsibly toward others, we first must be free to care for ourselves as persons.

4. Some permit themselves to be driven compulsively by an overwhelming sense of responsibility to an amazing array of needs.

At the other end of the balance scale from those who shirk responsibility we find those harried, tense souls who rush around from one meeting to another, who add project to project until at last they collapse on a hospital bed with ulcers or a heart attack. They have not learned to come to grips with reality. We *are* limited. We cannot meet every need. They also have not learned to trust others with responsibility. And they have not learned to delineate between the difference of remaining sensitive and open to all need without feeling compelled to respond personally to each call for help. Which leads us to our next point.

5. A more acceptable way to handle responsibility.

Jesus points the way for us to respond to need. He saw need on a much wider scope than we ever do. The bruises and wounds of those he loved twisted and knotted his stomach. But as he pointed out need to his followers, he also told them how to respond. "The harvest is plenteous," he said. "The fields are white. But the laborers are few. Pray, therefore, the Lord of the harvest that he will thrust forth laborers into the harvest."

An appropriate and effective response then to overwhelming need is not to shirk it, not to shut it out, not to become calloused or indifferent, not to lose our joy through a sense of frustration, not to walk around with a burdened, hangdog look because of guilt, but rather we respond by turning over the need to God. He is far more concerned than we. We ask him to fill the needs, to call forth workers. Of course, as we pray we will hold ourselves open to anything he has to say to us.

In the last chapter of this book we shall consider more specifically just how we can ascertain wherein our specific personal responsibilities lie, but we shall touch on four guidelines in this chapter also.

How Do We Know to Which Needs We Should Respond?

Guideline No. 1. We have to be convinced the need actually exists. When Bernard Palmer, well-known author, and his wife,

Marge, really began to believe some of their relatives were not Christians (they saw very little in life or conversation to indicate this), they began to pray for them. One by one they prayed for them and loved them and, as there was occasion, helped them. The result has been that the last I heard 28 of their relatives definitely have committed their lives to Christ. But the beginning of that ministry was acceptance of the fact that the relatives needed to come to know Christ personally.

Guideline No. 2. Sometimes other people will call to our attention a need to which we can respond. This was true of Bert and Mary of Los Angeles. It all began when their daughter, Sharon, after a year and a half in college, came home and announced, "I want to get away and think. I'm going to Mexico Saturday. There's an orphanage there where I want to work."

And Sharon told her parents about the Christian couple who had taken in one or two homeless waifs first, and then more and more children had come until they had more to care for than they could manage on their own. With mixed feelings Mary watched Bert and Sharon drive off on Saturday. When Bert came back, she questioned him and then said, "I want to go and see for myself."

Those who have crossed the U.S. border into Baja, California, know the depressed feeling that comes when you are confronted with miserable shacks, junk everywhere, mud roads and bare hills. "As we drove into the yard of the orphanage, my heart sank," Mary recalls. "The sickly, sweet smell of urine greeted us. As a nurse I guessed the smell was coming from more than the outdoor privys, and later found I was right. The children, who had been mistreated before coming to the orphanage, wet their beds.

" 'You need plastic mattress covers,' I said to Sharon.

" 'No money, Mom,' she said.

"On the way home my heart was perplexed. 'Lord,' I prayed, 'I know we gave our daughter to you, but why did you have to send her to such a place?' And do you know what the Lord answered me? He said, 'Quit your belly-aching and get down there and help her.'

140

"Shortly after I addressed a women's gathering. I told them about the need of the orphanage. Good used mattresses were donated. I sewed plastic mattress covers with muslin backing that slipped on like pillow cases. Then we loaded the car with food and again visited the orphanage. Oh, how grateful they were! You see, they had had only beans for 3 weeks.

"Word spread about the orphanage. Members from one of our churches visited it. They asked Sharon what her greatest need was. She rolled up the sleeves of her blouse. Her arms were peppered with large, red welts. 'Bedbugs,' she said simply. 'Can you do anything about them?'

"They hired a Mexican firm to fumigate once a month, and so got rid of the bugs. The church also supplied wool blankets, toilets, heaters, a bathtub, food, clothing, and much more.

"My husband collected and repaired old washing machines. I collected used clothing. Many church people and groups became interested. It was thrilling to see many needs met and improvements taking place. For almost two years every spare hour of ours was poured into the orphanage. Then our daughter felt she should return to college for further training. Individuals and groups still help the orphanage, and so the work continues. How happy we are for the experience we had! We've never been the same since, and we wouldn't have missed it for anything."

Sharon uncovered the need for her parents, and they, in turn, were able to communicate the need to others.

Guideline No. 3. Often God makes his will clear to us through open and closed doors.

Edner and Fern Holmen, a farming couple in Butterfield, Minnesota, cherished an intense interest in missions. This led to their beginning to prepare themselves by getting further training and then offering themselves for service overseas. But when Fern's heart condition closed the door for them they turned back to their 273-acre mortgaged farm and waited on God for further directions. By living simply and setting goals for giving, in two decades they have been able to give over $40,000, and their giving currently exceeds a fourth of their income. Closed doors to one area of service opened other doors even wider.

Guideline No. 4. When we say we are open to all needs but respond to "opportunities at hand," we mean opportunities we have the skills and abilities to meet.

John and Polly Holloway were in their forties when they took off for Tanzania, East Africa. In addition to years of business experience, John had a CPA certificate tucked away and the understanding of the Bible that had come through 14 Bible correspondence courses. John used his skills to work as a business manager and field treasurer for the Lutheran Church of Tanzania, and in his "spare" time preached and taught and planted a church.

After four years in Tanzania they went to Ecuador to oversee the finances of a large school built mainly with a grant from Germany's Bread for the World funds. In Ecuador too John planted a church.

John and Polly, currently in Hawaii, are quick to acknowledge they couldn't have done what they did without the loyal support of the congregation from which they came, Bethel of Shoreline in Seattle. The combined abilities and resouces of the Holloways and their congregation made it possible for them to respond to opportunities which presented themselves.

Guideline No. 5. We might see need and opportunities for which we presently do not have resources, but that need not deter us. God can provide resources in many ways.

When Art Storhaug of Larkspur, a suburb of San Francisco, wanted to go to Tanzania under World Brotherhood Exchange, he lacked the funds needed to transport his family to Africa. That did not stop Art. He borrowed the needed money. At the end of their term when they flew back to the U.S.—again on borrowed money—Art's wife, Esther, thought they were back to stay. But, no. As soon as Art had his loan paid off, he offered his services to the Lutheran World Federation. There was an opening to work in the Tanzania Christian Refugee Service in Dar es Salaam. In 1975 when they return to the States they will have completed an eight-year stay in East Africa. As Art has been busy caring for the thousands of refugees that flood into Tanzania, Esther has found joy in teaching the Bible during released time in the schools. This last term she also has worked on an occupational therapy project for lepers, launching a garden and chicken project. New life and hope have come to the leper patients as they have been able to earn an income selling eggs and broiler chickens.

Even as Art and Esther discovered, we too shall experience that as we launch out and use the resources we have, God supplies the ones we need but lack.

We should interject, before we leave the subject of missions, that changing times and conditions are altering the traditional pattern of missions. In many places "mission fields" have ceased to exist. The church of Jesus Christ has taken root and is growing. Leaders are springing up within the national churches. Revival and renewal stimulate generous giving and the Christians are assuming support of the work. But need for trained personnel in many areas of work continues to exist. So the emphasis has shifted from work in a definite church-governed field to supplying needed personnel for projects of the existing national churches. Intercristo, a computer style service, facilitates the matching of need with personnel for many church groups.

If you have a skill you would like to use overseas, contact the personnel director of the overseas work of your church. He will be able to tell you if there are any openings and guide you as to how to proceed.

Saying "Yes" Enriches Us

As we in our middle years realize that the "good life" is not to be equated merely with comfort, material possessions, freedom, leisure, or security, we shall be freed to act responsibly, which is the essence of assuming responsibility. By-products will be satisfaction, inner peace, personal growth, broadened understanding, and a softening of our hearts with compassion. And all of this, even though we may face difficult trials, will make the years ahead the best years we've had.

To Think About

How can I, as a Christian, act responsibly in regard to my-

143

self, my immediate family, my extended family, my friends, my church, my community, the world at large?

In addition to our individual, personal acts of love and concern, we can act responsibly by being members of organizations. Ask yourself:

- To what organizations do I belong?
- What is their purpose?
- What do they accomplish?
- How do they benefit my family? My community?
- What is my responsibility within that organization?
- Are there other organizations which have more meaningful goals than the ones to which I presently belong?
- During the past two years have I been influential in bringing about change or reform in any area where it is really needed?

12

Keeping Green

> *Maturity: among other things — not to hide one's strength out of fear and, consequently, live below one's best.*
>
> —DAG HAMMARSKJOLD

We were seated at the table for dinner. Our guest was a young man who was graduating from college in a week's time. "Only seven more days," he exulted, "and I'll be free! No more hassle with school or books."

One of our youngsters stared at him, her fork arrested halfway in its journey to her mouth. "No more school?" she asked. "Never?"

"Never!"

She regarded his bright young face with wonder, then looked at our beginning-to-gray heads and shook her head. "Can you beat that?" she said. "I thought people went to school and studied all their lives. My mom and dad do."

Luverne and I are, of course, only two of a steadily growing number of adults returning to school, 13 million at last count (not including full-time students). Or as the *U.S. News and World Report* states, 1 adult of every 8 is going to classes of some kind.

What Lures People Back to the Classroom?

Psychologists tell us *one of the needs of middle adulthood is cognitive.* One person explained it this way: "I feel a lot more learning facility in middle life than I did when I was in high school and college. I have a desire to learn new things, to read more books, to be creative. I am far more stimulated than I was when I was younger."

But usually we do not think in terms of satisfying a basic human need when we return to the classroom. Instead we are more apt to give other reasons.

If we are in business or some profession, the explosion of knowledge we are experiencing makes it necessary for us to take courses periodically in order *to update our skills and not become obsolete.*

A family counselor told me that in her field, between the years 1900–1965, 13,880 research articles on the family were published by 7000 authors, and in the U.S. and Canada over 700 different books on the family can be found on the shelves in libraries. Imagine the difficulty of keeping abreast of all that knowledge! The same is true in other fields as well. And it is anticipated that in this next decade knowledge will double.

Many of those back in school are men, *preparing themselves for a second or third career.* A retired navy officer we know is employed in an executive position now, but is taking a CPA course in preparation for a third career.

Hundreds of the middle-aged students are *women who are preparing themselves for employment outside the home.* No longer content to work as sales clerks or waitresses, they are training to do the work they've always wanted to do. "Only one more year, and I'll have my degree in nursing," one radiant woman told me. "The dream of a lifetime about to be fulfilled."

Others are thinking ahead to retirement years when they will have large chunks of time to fill up. They are discovering and developing skills and interests: writing, painting, music, ceramics, sewing.

Some study for the love of learning. Possessed with an eager, inquisitive mind, they are always rejoicing over horizons broadened and the dawning of new understanding. "I never realized before how little I really know," one soon-to-retire business man, who has registered for a number of history courses, told me.

A few seek companionship and friendship among like-minded

146

people in the classes they attend. Enrolled in a psychology class I took was a woman who had just suffered a divorce. She found the receptive friendliness and concern of her young fellow students healing.

Whatever their reason, middle-aged Americans are on the march back to school. And the doors are wide open. No longer is the complaint, "I wish I had been able to get more education" valid. It's never too late. Even 60-, 70- and 80-year-olds are realizing this.

In 1971 North Hennepin State Junior College in suburban Minneapolis decided to offer tuition-free classes specifically designed for those 55 and over. More than 400 enrolled. In a year's time that number doubled.

France's Third Age College in Toulouse, a division of the University of Toulouse, enrolled over 1000 students during their first year. Half were in their 60s. Another 35% are in their 70s and 80s, and three students are in their 90s. At Fairhaven College in Bellingham, Washington, 33 adults aged 60 to 80 are paying modest fees to live on campus in a dormitory. In addition to auditing classes and attending lectures and concerts, the oldsters are helping in the day-care center and providing valuable guidance and perspective for their younger campus neighbors. If oldsters are doing this, what should middle-agers be able to do?

New Opportunities for Study

About 50 miles down the freeway from where we live is Hollywood Community Adult School (Hollywood High School by day). Every year 10,000 adults register there and study over 100 different subjects. Thousands of high schools offer similar programs. Colleges and universities across the land welcome the mature student, either as day or night students.

Consider new patterns emerging. Take Brooklyn College. Brooklyn College now gives adults credits for life experience. For example, Bill Powers, 36, was one of their students. When Bill applied at Brooklyn he spoke one dialect of Sioux fluently and had published a number of works on American Indian culture. He also spoke three other languages: Spanish, French, and Italian. He was editorial promotion director of *Boys' Life* magazine. He also had sung with a professional vocal group and had acted in the theater. These life experiences added up to 54 college credits. Powers did so well in his studies he was able to work simultaneously on a B.A. and also an M.A. program at Wesley University in Connecticut.

Brooklyn College is not alone. Antioch College pioneered in giving credits for life experience. Since then more than 50 colleges have joined the University of Michigan, Radcliffe, and Sarah Lawrence in designing curricula for women after they have raised their families.

In Britain more than 25,000 students attend Britain's Open University on a day-to-day basis simply by switching on their radio or TV sets. A B.A. can be earned in 3 years at a cost of less than $400. Students study not less than 10 hours a week and attend a one- or two-week summer school, followed by terminal examinations. The radio and TV lessons are integrated with written material sent to the student's home.

Similarly the U.S. Office of Education is experimenting with the University without Walls, a $415,000 venture, launched by a consortium of 19 colleges.

Even in Senegal, Africa, TV is being utilized for adult education programs. TV sets are not numerous, so clubs are formed where all members view the program.

In 1973 here in the U.S. an adult career education color TV series went on the air in rural and urban areas in 14 states. Radio, print, telephone, and personal contact will be used to bring career education to adults in their homes.

The Institute of Lifetime Learning has eight institutes in major cities and fledgling branches in 40 more. The Institute in Washington, D.C., enrolls 9000 in 80 different courses. Members pay a reasonable fee for the courses.

Then there are learning labs, which have programed materials that users can select to learn at their own pace.

Nor does one have to go to school in order to keep green. Libraries are well-stocked with books, records, tapes, films. The

148

Long Beach California City Library even loans out framed prints of famous paintings for people to hang in their home and enjoy for a month.

In addition, YMCAs, churches, civic groups and other organizations sponsor courses too. Many of these are practical, designed to help in the art of living. Courses in marriage and family relationships and money management are becoming more and more common.

Pastor Ray Flachmeier of Ascension Lutheran Church, Garland, Texas, offers courses in transactional analysis. The courses are six 2-hour sessions held weekly. He uses as his texts *Born to Win* by James and Jongward, *Sex in Human Loving* and *What Do You Say After You Say Hello?* by Eric Berne; *Games Alcoholics Play* by Claude M. Steiner. The ideas and techniques he has received from several friends who are TA psychiatrists, counselors, and consultants. In addition to teaching members of his own congregation, Pastor Flachmeier once had a class of 22 from Humble Oil Corporation comprised of executives and their wives.

Going Back to School Full-time

"I might be able to manage a course or two like that," you say, "but to do what I really want to do I would need to go full-time for four years. Impossible!"

Maybe not. Admittedly it's difficult for a man, although many manage by going to night school several years. If you're a woman, it can be done a bit more easily. Oh, it still won't be easy, but the satisfaction gained is usually worth the effort many times over. At least this is what Kay Lee of Rowland Heights, California, says. Kay approached middle age with the dissatisfied feeling that she had not accomplished all she had hoped to, that she could do more if only she were better trained.

Before marriage Kay had earned a Bachelor of Sacred Music degree. After college she married a young pastor, Otis Lee. Giving birth to and raising five children as she followed her husband first to Alaska and then to Brazil filled the next 25 years.

Any spare time she filled with teaching and home study and gloried in both. But she longed for the challenge and discipline of a classroom situation, the insight of an authority and interaction with other learners. A dream she had cherished of teaching kindergarten began to flicker to life. But training would mean returning to college. Why not? Otis said. So when the Lees returned to the U.S. from Brazil, both Kay and a son registered as students at Biola College in La Mirada, California.

Their son lived on campus. With one daughter still in junior high, one in high school, a busy pastor-husband and a bedridden mother to care for, Kay commuted the 11 miles from their home 3 days a week. She applied for and received a student loan through a bank.

"I looked forward to each class hour," Kay says. "History brought new appreciation of great men of the past. Philosophy opened new vistas of thought. Art appreciation was a joy."

But math was Kay's downfall! Her struggle with basic math produced only a dismal D and brought Kay's grade point average down to a 3.35 when she had hoped for a top score. Kay encountered math again in a statistics course during her third year. The course was required for the psychology major Kay hoped to earn. At first Kay stubbornly said to herself, "If all these kids can do it, I can too." But as the classes became increasingly difficult, Kay decided to work around her problem by changing her major to humanities. Immediately she found herself in her element, and each class a challenge and joy.

During her second year her mother died. Kay increased her load to 15 and 18 units a semester. Outside of school Kay narrowed down her life to only the essentials. But she included in those "essentials" Sunday school teaching, choir directing, some home visitation, and an hour a week for group Bible study.

Kay's family was supportive. Her married daughters were proud their mother was at college. Kay found her own understanding widening. New insights provided lines of communication with the growing young adults of their family. Mealtime conversation perked up, and food was seasoned with a lively exchange of ideas that flew across the table. As Kay gained knowledge, her self-confidence grew. At the same time she became more aware of the problems and pressures her children were facing. Her children sensed this and began to express their fears as well as sharing their successes.

Graduation day her family applauded as Kay walked off the stage, not only with her B.A. degree, but a cum laude recognition.

You Can Too

So if you feel God calling you to a particular work but lack the training, take courage from Kay. Knowing what you want, combined with experience, perseverance and patience can see your dream realized. No matter what your needs are, your chances of finding a course are excellent. Check the public library. If you are employed, inquire as to whether your company will sponsor education for you either through released-time programs or by paying tuition courses.

If you live in a rural community or are a shut-in, you can study by correspondence. Opportunities for discovering and developing our abilities in these middle years never have been as plentiful. Use them!

The Superintendent of Documents, Washington, D.C., 20402, has a pamphlet on *Continuing Education Programs and Services for Women,* a state-by-state report of what's available.

For information on the program of the Institute of Lifetime Learning, write 215 Long Beach Blvd., Long Beach, Ca. 90801, or, Suite 601, Dupont Circle Bldg., 134C Connecticut Ave. N.W., Washington, D.C. 20036.

Correspondence courses offered by private home-study schools are described in a free directory from National Home Study Council, 1601 Eighteenth St. N.W., Washington, D.C., 20009.

National University Extension Association, Suite 360, One Dupont Circle, Washington, D.C., 20036, has a booklet listing universities and colleges and the courses they offer.

13

Setting Goals

"A goal is like a magnet. It motivates a person, directs his behavior and brings out his best performance."

—Dr. George Haddad

I was sitting on the floor with my young fellow student friends in Psychology 1-A class at Cypress College. Our class had divided into groups to study the different developmental stages of man. The group reporting had chosen to study the middle years. They had conducted surveys, going up and down their blocks asking people questions.

"We asked them what their goals are now," one of the girls said. "Their children are on their own or soon will be. Their home is nearly paid for. They still have several years left before retirement. They seemed surprised. 'Goals? Well, uh . . .' they stuttered, 'Dunno, hadn't thought much about it.' Fish a little, maybe, camp a little, travel a little; they didn't know really, hadn't thought too much about it."

"We asked them if they were happy," another boy reported. "They sort of stared at me when I asked. Happy? Happy? What was happiness? Why, sure they s'posed they were happy. Wife hasn't left them yet. Kids married. Job going all right. Retirement benefits stacking up. Health reasonably good. Why shouldn't they be happy?"

One of the girls interrupted. "I think that they're still all shook up because they've been left on their own. Kids are gone. What's there left to live for?"

"I know," one of the long-haired youth said thoughtfully. "It's so sad. There just aren't any of us kids who are worthy of the entire lifetime of two individuals. I mean, if all they have lived for is us, their children, how can we hope to become so great that their investment of two entire lives will be justified? Really, they should have something else to live for besides us. Some other goals and concerns—especially in this day and age."

In my place in the circle I sat silent, but listened so hard I was sure my ears, like a rabbit's, must be poking up through my hair.

That was the beginning of my inquiry. Are the young people correct in their observations, I wondered. Are we really living without goals? I began to listen, to ask questions, to read. The final outcome is this book. And now we have come to the closing chapter, our final visit together.

We have noted so far that midway through life we acknowledge, with thankfulness:

- that we are the recipients of bonus years, a longer span of middle years, replete with opportunities, than has ever been known before by a generation or civilization
- that God holds out to us the promise of a life that brings infinite satisfaction
- that research and good living conditions have granted us better physical health and a longer life than has ever been true before
- that much help is available to teach us to cope with and use creatively tensions and pressures
- that even pain and disability, when encountered and handled aright, can lead us to fuller lives
- that married life, after 15 or 20 years, can become richer, happier than it ever has been
- that new relationships with young adult children can bring joy as we experience how rewarding it is to be able to enjoy the delightful people our children have become
- that even if our children bring heartaches, still God's sustaining grace is available for us
- that an amazing army of concerned people stand by to help us care lovingly for aging parents

154

- that, at long last, we are beginning to understand that security, like satisfaction, does not lie in the dollar, but in the unshakeable certainty, based on God's word, that God will not abandon us
- that we have not peaked out—adventure still beckons us
- that assuming responsibility will make all we have gone through so far infinitely worthwhile as we find opportunities to use all we have learned and earned
- that it is possible for us to get whatever training we need to accomplish the goals we set
- that we are not left on our own. All the resources of God are available for us. We can live a God-directed, purposeful life with worthwhile, significant goals.

Impressive as this list is, still these facts are not the most important considerations. The most important issue is couched in a question. What are we going *to do* with all this?

Setting New Goals

One of the purposes of this book has been to help us think back over the way we have come, reevaluate goals we set earlier in life and set new goals for the last half of our lives.

How can we choose wisely our goals? Or we can rephrase the question by asking, how can we know God's will and plan for our lives?

Here are some suggested steps of action. They have helped me again and again in understanding God's will for me. Perhaps they will be of help to you.

As Christians, our position is unique. We may expect God to guide us. Therefore our procedure in arriving at goals will be different from that found in secular books on the subject.

1. As a Christian, I shall begin my search by making a commitment or recommitment of myself to God. I give myself to him. I promise to obey him in whatever I believe he wants me to do.

Often it is helpful to make this commitment in writing; then we are decisive about it. Writing is also useful because then we can return to our written pact with God, reread it and reaffirm our stance during days of temptation and indecision. For your guidance, a suggested statement of commitment is included at the end of this chapter.

Some of us may get hung up on this first step. It is not easy to give ourselves to God. The root of sin, which basically is an independent spirit which desires to live apart from God, is buried deep within us. Selfishly we may be glad to experience the release from guilt which comes when we accept the forgiveness of God. But to surrender *all* our "rights" to God—well, that's a different matter!

To give ourselves entirely to God is difficult also because sin has warped our thinking. In our crooked way we envision God's will for us to be something unpleasant, undesirable, difficult—a cross to be borne. We have a hard time believing God's will for us will be joyous, easy to bear, bringing us the utmost in satisfying fulfillment in life. Because of our warped outlook, we shrink back from making a commitment of ourselves to God.

I was 19 when the Lord showed me how shallow my first commitment to him had been, and how sweeping and inclusive he wanted it to be. It stunned me, frightened me. "If I give God my eyes," I foolishly worried, "suppose he takes my eyesight from me?" Fear controlled me. I needed love to motivate me and trust to take the leap.

Indeed, only as we grow in love and trust of our Heavenly Father will we be able to make ever deeper commitments to him. It should be an ongoing process. All too often it isn't. The flame of devotion and dedication burns white-hot during youth, only to cool off gradually until by mid-life we can rationalize the rightness of our choosing to what extent we shall obey God. We become wise in our own discernment. Wedded to security, we are governed by fear instead of being motivated by love. That is why it is good, midway in life, to pause and make a commitment of ourselves to God. The decisive act should be followed by a day-to-day and hour-to-hour reaffirmation to God and ourselves that Jesus indeed is Lord, and we are his.

So by making a covenant of obedience with God we establish our ultimate goal for life. From there we can move on to re-

156

ceive directions for secondary goals which will be accomplished in longer or shorter periods of time.

In understanding what our secondary goals should be, we need God's guidance. How can we know what to pursue? Having told God we are ready to follow his leading, here are the next steps we can take.

2. Set aside at least 10 minutes every day for two weeks when quietly and without interruption you can think, pray and listen. When you get an inkling of some goal you believe God wants you to set, write it down. Some goals will be short-term. Others long-range. Some will be for personal growth. Others for service. Review the goals suggested as you read this book.

3. At the end of two weeks, sit down and make out three lists. On one, list all your abilities. On the other, list your developed skills. (Many universities offer tests to help you evaluate your abilities and skills.) On the third list write down your weaknesses.

There are two reasons for taking into consideration our weaknesses. In the first place, deep within ourselves we want most to succeed where we are weak. We want to turn our weaknesses into strengths. God understands this. He seems to delight in calling us to tasks that seem too big for us, in order that his power and enabling may be manifest in our lives. If we let God transform weaknesses into strengths, after our goals are accomplished, we can sit back and marvel and even chuckle a bit, because we *know we* haven't done it; it has been God at work through us.

Secondly, as we write down our weaknesses, we can take a good square look at them. We can ask ourselves why we are weak in these particular points. In many cases we are weak because someone has told us so often that we can't do a particular thing that we actually believe it. We maybe haven't even *tried.*

In my youth some friends and I were renovating some rooms. One of us was handy with the saw; she did all the carpentry. I drew up the decorating plans and made the slipcovers for the furniture. A third girl did the painting. I wanted to help her, but she steadfastly refused, saying I wouldn't do a good enough job. Instead I was assigned the task of sanding down all the dribble marks from previous paint jobs.

The conviction that I could not do a good job painting became so strong for me that it was only recently I dared pick up a paint brush and try. I discovered, with joy, that with care and attention, I could indeed paint.

So it is well to consider our weaknesses and ask if they are real or just boogey-men, figments of our imagination.

4. Take your three lists to a friend (or friends) who knows you well. Ask if he has any additions. Often we are not aware of all the gifts God has given us. Someone close to us can see us more clearly.

5. Now go back and look over your list of desired goals and your lists of abilities, acquired skills, and weaknesses. Can you see how they fit together?

6. We do best cutting life into sizeable chunks we can handle. To attempt too much only produces frustration and discouragement. So, for now, from your list of goals select five short-term and two long-term goals. From the five short-term choose two and from the two long-term goals select only one. Write down these three goals on an index card. Carry it with you. Write the other four goals on another card and put these in your drawer. These are for you to hold in readiness in the back of your mind, so as soon as you have accomplished one of the first goals, you can launch out on another. This is important, for the pursuit of a goal is perhaps more fascinating and rewarding than the actual accomplishment of the goal, and we need something to capture our enthusiasm as soon as a goal is won. Otherwise we are apt to experience a sag and maybe even depression.

Now if you are having difficulty knowing, for example, what goals to set which will call for your time and energy, here is a practical bit of advice. Begin by doing whatever you find at hand waiting to be done. "Whatever your hand finds to do, do it with all your might," is a good rule to follow. If you can't see anything to do, go to your pastor, the principal of your local school, the local volunteer bureau, the mayor of your city or any philanthropic-minded leader of the community and ask if they have any openings where they can use you. Often as we become involved, we will find something that will really grab us.

When this happens, go back to your lists. Compare again. Interest alone is not enough. Ability should match interest. For example, being a doctor fascinates me. But I question whether I have the ability.

However, let us say ability does match interest. But skills are needed also and you have not yet developed the skills. Do not let this deter you. Skills can be developed. However, as you consider this aspect, you need to be realistic and sensible. For example, even if I decided to test and see whether or not I have the ability to become a doctor, still for me, at my age, to launch out on the required study program surely would not be feasible. So although medicine interests me, I rule it out. As I consider the skills I need to develop, I take into consideration the length of time it will take to develop the skills and whether or not enough years will be left afterwards to make the time of preparation spent worthwhile.

7. When you begin to get a sense of direction, talk it over with your family. Working toward your goals may cost them something. Are they happy with your projected plans?

8. A life with goals usually means a narrowed-down and disciplined life. You will have to weed out activities that have little or no meaning. You also will have to say 'no' to valid calls for service. Are you prepared for this?

9. Once involved, don't be surprised when testings and discouragements attack you. They will only confirm your calling. If your motivation is God's call to you, the only thing that will really matter to you is your obedience. Don't be afraid of failure. You might not succeed in all your goals; you very likely won't. But at least you've had fun trying, and what you have learned can help you attain your next goal.

10. Periodically, every three or six months, for example, review your goals. Do you still consider them worthwhile? What progress have you made toward attaining them? Is it time to set new goals?

Faithfulness in little responsibilities doubtless will lead to something bigger. Stretch and grow. It is thus you will continue to satisfy the need for adventure at the same time as you will assume more and more responsibility. And you will discover that the bonus years of mid-life, rather than being aimless, drifting years, instead hold out indeed the promise of the best years to come.

MY COVENANT

My God, here am I. By your grace I give you my all. I understand this to be my body, mind and soul, my faculties and abilities, my time and future, my home, goods, and money, my family and loved ones, my position and ambitions, my likes and dislikes, my habits, my failures, my sins, and all other things of any nature that I have counted my own.

I lay this all on your altar and reckon it all from this moment on to be yours. Take me, cleanse me, live out your life through me.

During my pilgrimage on this earth, I recognize that you have given me all these things as a trust, and I reckon myself to be a steward of them. I do this all to advance your kingdom and to bring glory to your name. By your grace I shall rejoice to see this accomplished in whatever way you direct.

I commit my way unto you and trust you to lead me. I believe in you, I love you and I trust you, and I am confident that you are able to keep that which I have committed to you until I meet you face to face.